KU-524-922

Achieve great Chemistry with CGP!

Let's deal with the bad news first: the new Grade 9-1 GCSE Chemistry courses are tougher than ever, so you'll need to be at the top of your game on exam day.

Here's the good news: this fantastic CGP book is absolutely jam-packed with all the exam-style practice you'll need — it even covers all the new required practicals.

And since you'll be tested on a wide range of topics in the real exams, we've also included a section of mixed questions to keep you on your toes!

CGP — still the best! ☺

Our sole aim here at CGP is to produce the highest quality books — carefully written, immaculately presented and dangerously close to being funny.

Then we work our socks off to get them out to you — at the cheapest possible prices.

Contents

☑ Use the tick boxes to check off the topics you've completed.

Topic 8 — Fuels and Earth Science

Topic 9 — Separate Chemistry 2

Mixed Questions

Published by CGP

Editors:
Mary Falkner, Emily Forsberg, Paul Jordin, Sophie Scott.

Contributors:
Ian Davis, Chris Workman.

With thanks to Emily Howe and Jamie Sinclair for the proofreading.
With thanks to Ana Pungartnik for the copyright research.

Page 3 contains public sector information published by the Health and Safety Executive
and licensed under the Open Government Licence v3.0.
http://www.nationalarchives.gov.uk/doc/open-government-licence/version/3/

Page 95 contains public sector information licensed under the Open Government Licence v3.0.
http://www.nationalarchives.gov.uk/doc/open-government-licence/version/3/

Data used to construct the graph on page 95 provided by the JPL PODAAC, in support of the NASA's MEaSUREs program.

ISBN: 978 1 78294 496 6

Clipart from Corel®
Printed by Elanders Ltd, Newcastle upon Tyne

Based on the classic CGP style created by Richard Parsons.

Text, design, layout and original illustrations © Coordination Group Publications Ltd. (CGP) 2016.
All rights reserved.

Photocopying this book is not permitted. Extra copies are available from CGP with next day delivery.
0800 1712 712 • www.cgpbooks.co.uk

How to Use This Book

- Hold the book <u>upright</u>, approximately <u>50 cm</u> from your face, ensuring that the text looks like <u>this</u>, not s̄ı̄ɥ̄ʇ. Alternatively, place the book on a <u>horizontal</u> surface (e.g. a table or desk) and sit adjacent to the book, at a distance which doesn't make the text too small to read.

- In case of emergency, press the two halves of the book together <u>firmly</u> in order to close.

- Before attempting to use this book, familiarise yourself with the following <u>safety information</u>:

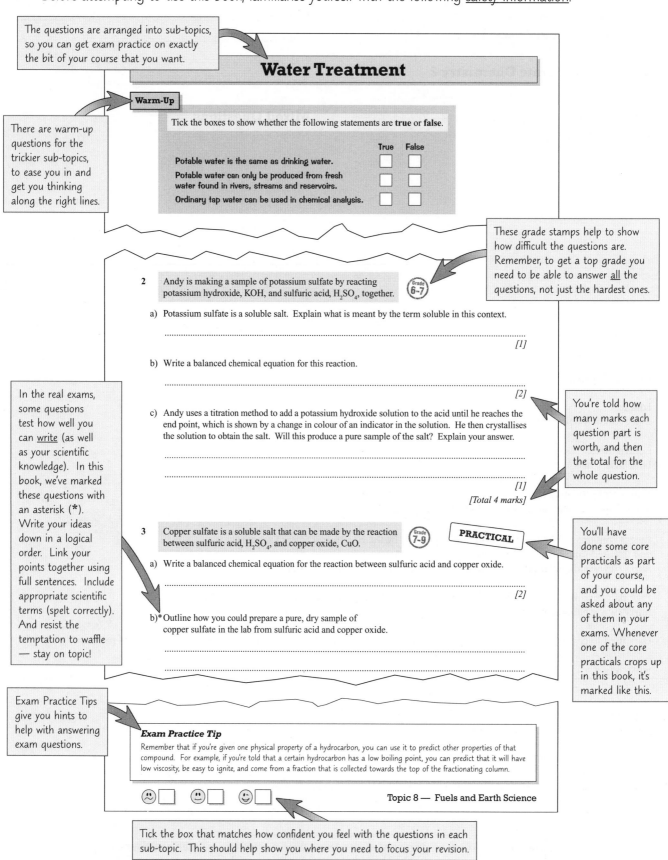

The questions are arranged into sub-topics, so you can get exam practice on exactly the bit of your course that you want.

There are warm-up questions for the trickier sub-topics, to ease you in and get you thinking along the right lines.

Water Treatment

Warm-Up

Tick the boxes to show whether the following statements are **true** or **false**.

	True	False
Potable water is the same as drinking water.	☐	☐
Potable water can only be produced from fresh water found in rivers, streams and reservoirs.	☐	☐
Ordinary tap water can be used in chemical analysis.	☐	☐

These grade stamps help to show how difficult the questions are. Remember, to get a top grade you need to be able to answer <u>all</u> the questions, not just the hardest ones.

2   Andy is making a sample of potassium sulfate by reacting potassium hydroxide, KOH, and sulfuric acid, H_2SO_4, together.   (Grade 6-7)

a) Potassium sulfate is a soluble salt. Explain what is meant by the term soluble in this context.

....
[1]

b) Write a balanced chemical equation for this reaction.

....
[2]

c) Andy uses a titration method to add a potassium hydroxide solution to the acid until he reaches the end point, which is shown by a change in colour of an indicator in the solution. He then crystallises the solution to obtain the salt. Will this produce a pure sample of the salt? Explain your answer.

....

....
[1]

[Total 4 marks]

You're told how many marks each question part is worth, and then the total for the whole question.

In the real exams, some questions test how well you can <u>write</u> (as well as your scientific knowledge). In this book, we've marked these questions with an asterisk (*****). Write your ideas down in a logical order. Link your points together using full sentences. Include appropriate scientific terms (spelt correctly). And resist the temptation to waffle — stay on topic!

3   Copper sulfate is a soluble salt that can be made by the reaction between sulfuric acid, H_2SO_4, and copper oxide, CuO.   (Grade 7-9)   **PRACTICAL**

a) Write a balanced chemical equation for the reaction between sulfuric acid and copper oxide.

....
[2]

b)* Outline how you could prepare a pure, dry sample of copper sulfate in the lab from sulfuric acid and copper oxide.

....

....

You'll have done some core practicals as part of your course, and you could be asked about any of them in your exams. Whenever one of the core practicals crops up in this book, it's marked like this.

Exam Practice Tips give you hints to help with answering exam questions.

Exam Practice Tip

Remember that if you're given one physical property of a hydrocarbon, you can use it to predict other properties of that compound. For example, if you're told that a certain hydrocarbon has a low boiling point, you can predict that it will have low viscosity, be easy to ignite, and come from a fraction that is collected towards the top of the fractionating column.

☹ ☐   ☺ ☐   ☺ ☐   Topic 8 — Fuels and Earth Science

Tick the box that matches how confident you feel with the questions in each sub-topic. This should help show you where you need to focus your revision.

Chemical Equations

1   Hydrogen gas is used as a reactant in the Haber Process. It can be made using the following reaction.

$$CH_4 + H_2O \rightarrow CO + 3H_2$$

Which of the following word equations correctly describes this reaction? Tick **one** box.

- [ ] **A** methane + water → carbon dioxide + hydrogen
- [ ] **B** ethane + water → carbon dioxide + hydrogen
- [✓] **C** methane + water → carbon monoxide + hydrogen
- [ ] **D** methane + water → carbon + oxygen + hydrogen

[Total 1 mark]

2   Calcium carbonate chips were reacted with nitric acid at room temperature. The products of the reaction were water, a gas and a salt solution.

Complete the reaction equation by adding state symbols to describe the reaction.

$$CaCO_3(..........) + 2HNO_3(..........) \rightarrow Ca(NO_3)_2(..........) + H_2O(..........) + CO_2(..........)$$

[Total 2 marks]

3   Sodium metal can react with oxygen molecules in the air to form sodium oxide (Na_2O).

Write a balanced equation for this reaction.

....

[Total 2 marks]

4   In a chemical reaction, sulfuric acid and aluminium metal react to form hydrogen gas and a salt solution of aluminium sulfate.

Ben has written this equation for the reaction:

$$Al_{(s)} + H_2SO_{4\,(aq)} \rightarrow Al_2(SO_4)_{3\,(aq)} + H_{2\,(g)}$$

a) Explain what is meant by the symbol '(aq)' in the chemical equation.

....

[1]

b) Ben's equation is not balanced. Write a balanced chemical equation for this reaction.

....

[1]

[Total 2 marks]

5   Nitric acid can be made using ammonia.

   a) The first stage in the manufacture of nitric acid is to oxidise ammonia, NH_3, to nitrogen(II) oxide, NO. Balance the equation for the reaction.

   .... NH_3 + ... O_2 → .... NO + ... H_2O

   [1]

   b) The reaction below shows the final stage in the manufacture of nitric acid. The equation is not balanced correctly. Explain how you can tell.

   $$2NO_2 + O_2 + H_2O → 2HNO_3$$

   ....

   ....

   [1]

   [Total 2 marks]

6   Silver chloride, AgCl, can be made by reacting silver nitrate, $AgNO_3$, and sodium chloride, NaCl, together in a precipitation reaction.

   $$AgNO_{3\,(aq)} + NaCl_{(aq)} → AgCl_{(s)} + NaNO_{3\,(aq)}$$

   a) How can you tell from the reaction equation that this is a precipitation reaction?

   ....

   [1]

   b) Write a balanced ionic equation for the reaction above.

   ....

   [2]

   [Total 3 marks]

7   Balance the following symbol equation to show how sulfur reacts with nitric acid.

   $$S + HNO_3 → H_2SO_4 + NO_2 + H_2O$$

   ....

   [Total 1 mark]

8   Zinc reacts with tin sulfate solution in a redox reaction. The full reaction equation is shown below.

   $$Zn_{(s)} + SnSO_{4\,(aq)} → ZnSO_{4\,(aq)} + Sn_{(s)}$$

   Write the ionic equation for the reaction above.

   ....

   [Total 2 marks]

Topic 1 — Key Concepts in Chemistry

Hazards and Risk

1 Eric is carrying out an experiment using some hazardous chemicals. One of the chemicals is stored in a flask, marked with the label shown in **Figure 1**.

Grade 4-6

Figure 1

a) Which of the following hazards are associated with the contents of the flask? Tick **one** box.

☐ **A** oxidising   ☐ **C** harmful

☐ **B** corrosive   ☐ **D** highly flammable

[1]

b) Suggest **one** safety precaution that Eric should take when using the chemical from the flask.

....

[1]

[Total 2 marks]

2 A lab technician is cleaning up a lab after an experiment. The experiment involved using chemicals from flasks marked with the label shown in **Figure 2**.

Grade 6-7

With reference to **Figure 2**, explain why the technician needs to be careful when disposing of the chemicals.

Figure 2

....

....

[Total 2 marks]

3* A student is planning an experiment to assess how the rate of a certain reaction changes with concentration. The reaction involves her using chemicals that are marked as harmful and corrosive. It also produces a gas.

Grade 7-9

Construct a risk assessment to outline the hazards associated with the experiment and the safety precautions that the student should take to reduce them.

....

....

....

....

....

....

....

[Total 6 marks]

Topic 1 — Key Concepts in Chemistry

The History of the Atom

Warm-Up

Draw **one** line from each atomic model to the correct description of that model.

Atomic Model

Plum pudding model

Bohr's model

Rutherford's nuclear model

Description

A positively charged 'ball' with negatively charged electrons in it.

A small, positively charged nucleus surrounded by a 'cloud' of negative electrons.

Electrons in fixed orbits surrounding a small, positively charged nucleus.

Solid spheres with a different sphere for each element.

1 Models of the atom have changed over time. **Grade 4-6**

Which of the following statements is the best description of what scientists thought an atom was like before the electron was discovered? Tick **one** box.

☐ **A** Tiny solid spheres that can't be divided.

☐ **B** Formless 'clouds' of matter.

☐ **C** Flat geometric shapes.

☐ **D** Discrete packets of energy.

[Total 1 mark]

2 In 1911, Rutherford, Geiger and Marsden carried out the gold foil experiment. They fired positively charged alpha particles at gold foil. They predicted that most of the particles would pass straight through the foil and a few might be deflected slightly. **Grade 6-7**

a) Describe what actually happened to the alpha particles during the gold foil experiment and explain why it happened.

....

....

....

....

[4]

b) Name the scientist who adapted Rutherford's nuclear model by suggesting that electrons orbit the nucleus at specific distances.

....

[1]

[Total 5 marks]

Topic 1 — Key Concepts in Chemistry

The Atom

1 **Figure 1** shows the structure of a certain atom. **Grade 4-6**

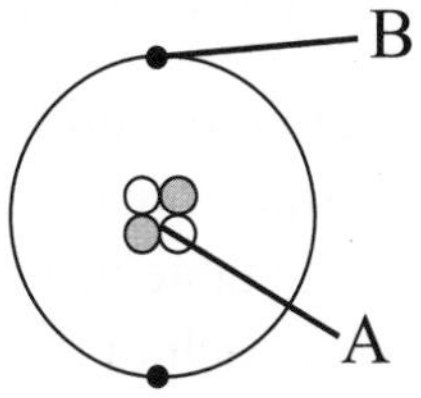

a) Name the region where most of the mass of the atom is concentrated.

....
[1]

Figure 1

b) What is the name of particle **B**?

....
[1]

c) State the **two** subatomic particles which are present in region **A**.

....
[1]

d) Use the relative charges of the subatomic particles to explain why an atom has no overall charge.

....

....

....

....
[3]

e) The atom shown in **Figure 1** has an atomic number of 2.
What is the name of the element that the atom in **Figure 1** makes up? Tick **one** box.

☐ **A** hydrogen   ☐ **B** lithium   ☐ **C** helium   ☐ **D** beryllium
[1]

[Total 7 marks]

2 A potassium atom can be represented by the nuclear symbol $^{39}_{19}K$. **Grade 4-6**

a) What is the mass number of $^{39}_{19}K$?

....
[1]

b) What is the atomic number of $^{39}_{19}K$?

....
[1]

c) How many protons, neutrons and electrons does an atom of $^{39}_{19}K$ have?

protons: ....   neutrons: ....   electrons: ....
[3]

[Total 5 marks]

Topic 1 — Key Concepts in Chemistry

Isotopes and Relative Atomic Mass

1   This question is about isotopes.

a) A neutral atom of sulfur, ^{32}S, has 16 electrons.
Sulfur has three other naturally occurring isotopes, with mass numbers 33, 34 and 36.
Complete the table in **Figure 1**, giving the number of protons, neutrons and
electrons for each of the naturally occurring isotopes of sulfur.

Isotope	Number of Protons	Number of Neutrons	Number of Electrons
^{32}S	....	....	16
^{33}S	....	....	....
^{34}S	....	....	....
^{36}S	....	....	....

Figure 1   *[3]*

b) Atom **X** has a mass number of 51 and an atomic number of 23.
Atom **Y** has a mass number of 51 and an atomic number of 22.
Atom **Z** has a mass number of 52 and an atomic number of 23.

Identify which pair of atoms are isotopes and explain why.

....

....

....

[3]

[Total 6 marks]

2   **Figure 2** shows some information about three isotopes of silicon.

Name	Atomic Number	Mass Number	Abundance (%)
Silicon-28	14	28	92.2
Silicon-29	14	29	4.70
Silicon-30	14	30	3.10

Figure 2

a) How many neutrons does an atom of silicon-29 contain?

neutrons = ...
[1]

b) Work out the relative atomic mass of silicon.

relative atomic mass = ...
[2]

[Total 3 marks]

3 Bromine has two main isotopes: Br-79 and Br-81. *(Grade 6-7)*

a) Give the definition of the term **isotopes**.

....

....
[1]

b) Bromine has an atomic number of 35. Calculate the number of neutrons in both isotopes.

Br-79 : .... neutrons

Br-81 : .... neutrons
[1]

c) The relative isotopic abundances of bromine-79 and bromine-81 are 12.67 and 12.32 respectively. Calculate the relative atomic mass of bromine. Give your answer to 2 significant figures.

relative atomic mass = ...
[2]

[Total 4 marks]

4 The relative atomic mass of every element can be found in the periodic table. *(Grade 6-7)*

a) Give the definition of the **relative atomic mass** of an element.

....

....
[2]

b) Explain why some elements have relative atomic masses that are not whole numbers.

....

....
[1]

[Total 3 marks]

5 Gallium can exist as two stable isotopes: Ga-69 and Ga-71. *(Grade 7-9)*

Give than 60.1% of gallium atoms are Ga-69 atoms, and the rest are Ga-71 atoms, calculate the relative atomic mass of gallium.

relative atomic mass = ...
[Total 3 marks]

Exam Practice Tip

Don't let isotopes confuse you. Just because they've got different numbers of neutrons, a pair of isotopes will still have the same number of protons, so they're still the same element. Those relative atomic mass calculations aren't too bad either. Remember — if your isotopic abundances are given as percentages, then they should always add up to 100%.

The Periodic Table

1 Chemical elements are arranged in the periodic table. **Grade 4-6**

a) How are the elements ordered in the modern periodic table?

....

[1]

b) Why do elements in groups have similar chemical properties? Tick **one** box.

☐ **A** They have the same number of shells of electrons.

☐ **B** They have the same number of outer shell electrons.

☐ **C** They all have at least one full inner shell of electrons.

☐ **D** The atoms of the elements are similar in size.

[1]

[Total 2 marks]

2 Mendeleev created an early version of the periodic table, in which he arranged the elements according to their atomic masses and their properties. Mendeleev left some gaps in his table. **Grade 6-7**

a) Explain why Mendeleev left gaps in his table.

....

....

[1]

b) Mendeleev used his table to predict the properties of undiscovered elements that would fit in the gaps he left. One of these was an element in Group 4, which Mendeleev called **eka-silicon**. **Figure 1** shows some properties of the Group 4 elements silicon and tin, plus some predictions about the properties of eka-silicon.

	Silicon (Si)	Eka-silicon (Ek)	Tin (Sn)
Atomic Mass	28	72	119
Density in g/cm³	2.3	?	7.3
Appearance	grey/silver non-metal	grey metal	grey metal
Formula of oxide	SiO_2	EkO_2	SnO_2
Formula of chloride	$SiCl_4$	?	$SnCl_4$
Reaction with acid	None	?	Slow

Figure 1

Use the information in **Figure 1** to predict the following properties of eka-silicon:

i) Density: ....

ii) Formula of chloride: ....

iii) Reaction with acid: ....

[3]

[Total 4 marks]

Topic 1 — Key Concepts in Chemistry

Electronic Configurations

1　The atomic number of neon is 10.　(Grade 6-7)

How many electrons does neon have in its **outer shell**?

☐ **A** 2　　　　☐ **C** 8

☐ **B** 6　　　　☐ **D** 10

[Total 1 mark]

2　The atomic number of sulfur is 16.　(Grade 6-7)

a) Write down the electronic structure of sulfur.

....

[1]

b) Draw a diagram to show how the electrons are arranged in a single sulfur atom.

[1]

[Total 2 marks]

3　Magnesium is found in group 2 and period 3 of the periodic table.　(Grade 6-7)

a) Explain how you could use this information to **deduce** the electronic structure of magnesium.

....

....

....

....

....

[3]

b) Give the electronic structure of magnesium.

....

[1]

[Total 4 marks]

Ions

Warm-Up

The formulas of the ion formed by four mystery elements are shown below. Draw lines to match each of the ions to the correct description of the element that it was formed from.

A⁺		A non-metal from Group 6
D⁻		A metal from Group 2
X²⁺		A metal from Group 1
Z²⁻		A non-metal from Group 7

1 Ions can have either a positive or a negative charge. *Grade 6-7*

a) Describe what happens to an atom when it turns into a negative ion.

....

[1]

b) Magnesium is in Group 2 of the periodic table.

i) Predict what charge a magnesium ion will have.

....

[1]

ii) Magnesium has the atomic number 12.
Calculate the number of electrons found in one magnesium ion.

number of electrons = ...

[1]

[Total 3 marks]

2 Potassium can react with oxygen to form the ionic compound potassium oxide. *Grade 7-9*

a) Which of following shows the correct formula for potassium oxide?

☐ **A** KO   ☐ **B** KO₂   ☐ **C** K₂O   ☐ **D** K₂O₂

[1]

b) The most common isotope of oxygen has an atomic number of 8 and a mass number of 16.
How many protons, neutrons and electrons would an oxide ion have?

protons = ...

electrons = ...

neutrons = ...

[3]

[Total 4 marks]

Topic 1 — Key Concepts in Chemistry

Ionic Bonding

1   Ionic bonding is one of the three types of chemical bonds found in compounds.   **Grade 4-6**

a) In which of the following compounds are the particles held together by ionic bonds?
Put a tick in the box next to the compound that you think is ionic.

     ☐   calcium chloride   ☐   carbon dioxide

     ☐   nitrogen monoxide   ☐   phosphorus trichloride

[1]

b) **Figure 1** shows the formation of the ionic compound lithium chloride from its elements, but it is incomplete. Complete **Figure 1** by drawing an arrow to show the transfer of the electron, adding the charges of the ions and completing the chloride ion to show the electrons in its outer shell.

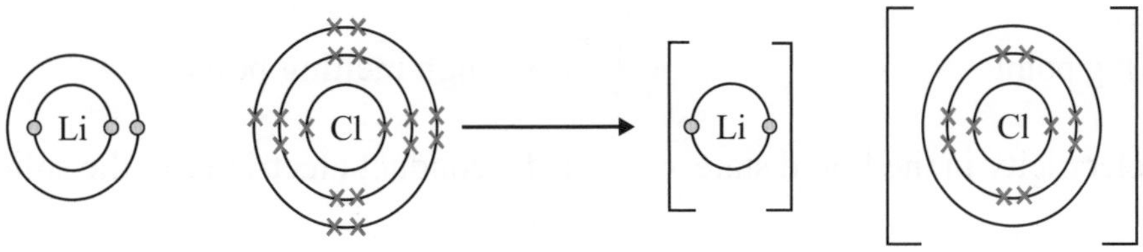

Figure 1

[3]

c) Name the force that holds the ions together in an ionic bond.

....

[1]

d) Suggest how you can tell from a dot and cross diagram that the
particles in a compound are held together by ionic bonds.

....

....

[1]

[Total 6 marks]

2   Calcium fluoride, CaF_2, is an ionic compound.   **Grade 6-7**

Draw a dot and cross diagram to show the bonding in calcium fluoride.
You should include the charges on the ions in your diagram.

[Total 4 marks]

Topic 1 — Key Concepts in Chemistry

Ionic Compounds

Circle the correct words or phrases below so that the statement is correct.

In an ionic compound, the particles are held together by <u>weak</u>/<u>strong</u> forces of attraction.

These forces act <u>in all directions</u>/<u>in one particular direction</u> which results in the particles

bonding together to form <u>giant lattices</u>/<u>small molecules</u>.

1   This question is about the structure and properties of ionic compounds.   (Grade 4-6)

a) Which of the following properties is **not** typical for an ionic compound?
Tick **one** box.

☐   **A** high boiling point   ☐   **C** high melting point

☐   **B** conduct electricity in the liquid state   ☐   **D** conduct electricity in the solid state

[1]

b) Name the type of structure that ionic compounds have.

....

[1]

[Total 2 marks]

2   Sodium chloride is an ionic compound.   (Grade 6-7)

a) Describe the structure of a crystal of sodium chloride. You should state:
   • What particles are present in the crystal.
   • How these particles are arranged.
   • What holds the particles together.

....

....

....

....

....

[4]

b) Explain why sodium chloride has a high melting point.

....

....

[2]

[Total 6 marks]

3 Potassium bromide has a lattice structure that is similar to sodium chloride.

a) Complete **Figure 1** below to show the position and charge of the ions in potassium bromide. Write a symbol in each blank circle to show whether it is a potassium ion or a bromide ion.

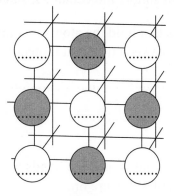

Figure 1

[3]

b) Give **one advantage** and **one disadvantage** of using the type of diagram above to represent the structure of an ionic compound.

Advantage: ....

Disadvantage: ....

[2]

c) State whether potassium bromide is likely to be **soluble** or **insoluble** in water.

....

[1]

[Total 6 marks]

4 **Figure 2** shows some data about the ionic compound lithium chloride. For each of the properties shown, explain how the structure of lithium chloride causes this property.

Boiling point / °C	Electrical conductivity of solid	Electrical conductivity of solution
1382	Low	High

Figure 2

Boiling point ....

....

....

Electrical conductivity of solid ....

....

Electrical conductivity of solution ....

....

[Total 6 marks]

Exam Practice Tip

Don't panic if you're asked about an ionic compound that you haven't met before. Think about what you <u>do</u> know about ionic compounds, and read the question carefully to make sure you've picked up on any extra information you've been given.

   Topic 1 — Key Concepts in Chemistry

Covalent Bonding

1 This question is about the forces in simple molecular substances. (Grade 4-6)

a) Compare the strength of the bonds that hold the atoms in a molecule together with the forces that exist between different molecules.

....

....

[2]

b) When a simple molecular substance melts, is it the bonds between atoms or the forces between molecules that are broken?

....

[1]

[Total 3 marks]

2 Silicon has the electronic structure 2.8.4. (Grade 6-7)

Use this information to predict how many covalent bonds one atom of silicon will form in a simple molecule. Explain your answer.

....

....

....

[Total 2 marks]

3 Nitrogen has the electronic structure 2.5. Chlorine has the electronic structure 2.8.7. Nitrogen trichloride, NCl_3, is a covalent compound. In each molecule of NCl_3, one nitrogen atom is covalently bonded to three chlorine atoms. (Grade 6-7)

a) Draw a dot and cross diagram to show the bonding in **one molecule** of nitrogen trichloride. You only need to include the outer shell electrons of each atom.

[3]

b) Predict, with reasoning, whether nitrogen trichloride can conduct electricity.

....

....

[1]

[Total 4 marks]

4 Hashim says: "Covalent bonds are very strong, so you need a lot of energy to separate the atoms in a covalent compound. This means simple molecular substances must have high melting and boiling points."

Grade 6-7

Is Hashim correct? Explain your answer.

....

....

....

....

....

....

[Total 3 marks]

5 Methane and poly(ethene) are both substances that are made up of molecules whose atoms are joined together by covalent bonds.

Grade 7-9

a) Briefly describe how the carbon and hydrogen atoms in methane, CH_4, bond to gain stable electronic structures.

....

....

....

....

[4]

b) What type of molecule is poly(ethene)?

....

[1]

c) At room temperature and pressure, methane is a gas, while poly(ethene) is a solid. Suggest why poly(ethene) has a higher boiling point than methane.

....

....

....

....

[4]

[Total 9 marks]

Exam Practice Tip

If you answered these questions correctly, then that's a pretty good sign that you know all about simple molecules and covalent bonding. But don't forget, that's only part of the story — you need to be able to compare simple molecular substances with all the other types of structure covered in this topic, such as ionic structures and giant covalent structures.

Topic 1 — Key Concepts in Chemistry

Giant Covalent Structures and Fullerenes

1 The diagrams below show two different types of carbon structure.

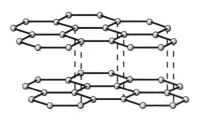

Figure 1   **Figure 2**

a) Name the two carbon structures shown.

   i) **Figure 1**: ....

                                                   [1]

   ii) **Figure 2**: ....

                                                   [1]

b) Both of the structures shown are able to conduct electricity.
Explain why this is possible.

   ....

   ....

   ....

                                                     [2]

c) Which of the two forms of carbon shown would you expect to have a **higher** melting point?
Explain your answer.

   ....

   ....

   ....

   ....

                                                     [3]

d) Name **one** other type of carbon structure, and draw a diagram below to show its bonding.

   Structure: ....

                                                     [2]

                                                    [Total 9 marks]

Metallic Bonding

1   This question is about how the structure and bonding of metals affects their properties.   Grade 6-7

a) Draw a labelled diagram to show how the metal ions and
the electrons that take part in bonding are arranged in a metal.

[3]

b) Explain how the metal ions are held together in this arrangement.

....

....
[2]

c) i) State whether metals generally have high or low boiling points. Explain your answer.

....

....
[2]

ii) A student has samples of two solids, marked **A** and **B**. One is copper, a metallic element, and
the other is iodine, a non-metal element. Solid **A** has a melting point of 1085 °C and solid **B**
has a melting point of 114 °C. Suggest which of the solids is iodine and explain your answer.

....

....
[1]

d) Explain why metals are good conductors of electricity.

....

....
[2]

e) Explain how the structure of metals means they are able to be bent and shaped.

....

....

....
[2]

[Total 12 marks]

Exam Practice Tip

Metals have some really nifty properties, and being able to explain all the properties of metals requires you to be really familiar with metallic bonding. Remember, it's because of those layers of positive metal ions and that sea of electrons that metals behave the way they do. Make sure you're able to explain the bonding in metals and link it to their properties.

 ☐   ☐   ☐   Topic 1 — Key Concepts in Chemistry

Conservation of Mass

1 A student mixes 3.0 g of silver nitrate solution and 15.8 g of sodium chloride solution together in a flask and seals it with a bung. The following precipitation reaction occurs:

$$AgNO_{3\,(aq)} + NaCl_{(aq)} \rightarrow AgCl_{(s)} + NaNO_{3\,(aq)}$$

Predict the total mass of the contents of the flask after the reaction. Explain your answer.

....

....

....

[Total 2 marks]

2 A student is investigating a reaction between zinc and hydrochloric acid. The reaction produces hydrogen gas and a solution of zinc chloride. The student's experimental set-up is shown in **Figure 1**.

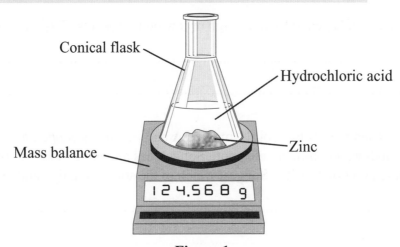

Figure 1

a) How would you expect the mass of the conical flask and its contents to change over the course of the reaction? Explain your answer.

....

....

....

[2]

b) The student repeats the reaction, but this time attaches a gas syringe to the top of the flask. How would you expect the mass of the apparatus and its contents to change over the course of the reaction? Explain your answer.

....

....

....

....

[2]

[Total 4 marks]

Relative Masses and Chemical Formulas

Match up the following formulas with the correct relative formula mass of the substance.

F_2		38
C_2H_6		40
CaO		30
NaOH		56

1 The compound butane-1,4-diamine has the molecular formula $C_4H_{12}N_2$. **Grade 4-6** Which of the following is the empirical formula of butane-1,4-diamine?

☐ **A** C_2H_5N ☐ **B** $C_2H_6N_2$ ☐ **C** CH_3N ☐ **D** C_2H_6N

[Total 1 mark]

2 Decaborane is a compound with the molecular formula $B_{10}H_{14}$. **Grade 4-6**

What is the empirical formula of decaborane?

empirical formula = ...
[Total 1 mark]

3 **Figure 1** shows the displayed formula of the compound dithionic acid. **Grade 4-6**

$$H-O-S-S-O-H$$

(with O double-bonded above and below each S)

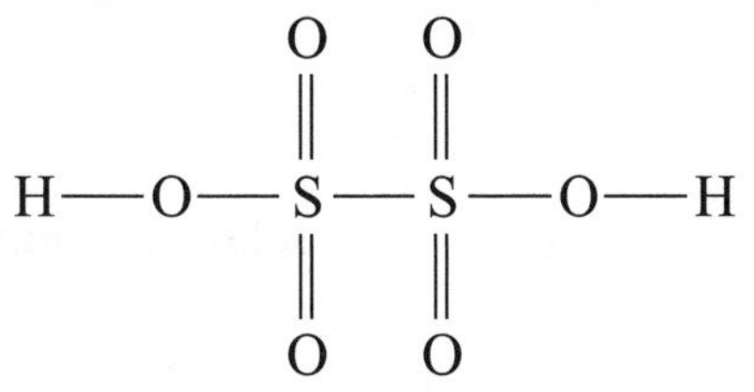

Figure 1

a) What is the molecular formula of this compound?
   Give your answer in the form $H_aS_bO_c$, where a, b and c are whole numbers.

....
[1]

b) What is the empirical formula of this compound?

empirical formula = ...
[1]

[Total 2 marks]

Topic 1 — Key Concepts in Chemistry

4 The formula of the compound barium nitrate is $Ba(NO_3)_2$.

Find the relative formula mass of barium nitrate.

relative formula mass = ...

[2]

5 Oct-1-ene is a compound with the molecular formula C_8H_{16}.
Emmy says the empirical formula of oct-1-ene is C_2H_4.

Is Emmy correct? Explain your answer.

....

....

....

[Total 1 mark]

6 An oxide of an element, X, has the formula X_2O_3.
The relative formula mass of X_2O_3 is 160.

Calculate the relative atomic mass of element X.

relative atomic mass = ...
[Total 3 marks]

7 Compound Q has the empirical formula C_2HF.
The relative formula mass of compound Q is 132.

What is the molecular formula of compound Q?

molecular formula = ...
[Total 3 marks]

Topic 1 — Key Concepts in Chemistry

Moles and Concentration

1   What is the approximate number of atoms in 1 mole of carbon atoms?   (Grade 4-6)

    ☐ **A** 7.23×10^{23} atoms   ☐ **C** 6.02×10^{-23} atoms

    ☐ **B** 7.23×10^{24} atoms   ☐ **D** 6.02×10^{23} atoms

[Total 1 mark]

2   A student makes a saline solution by dissolving 36 g of sodium chloride in 0.40 dm³ of water. What is the concentration of the solution?   (Grade 4-6)

    ☐ **A** 90 g dm⁻³   ☐ **B** 14.4 g dm⁻³   ☐ **C** 14 400 g dm⁻³   ☐ **D** 0.090 g dm⁻³

[Total 1 mark]

3   A pharmacist is synthesising aspirin, $C_9H_8O_4$, as part of a drugs trial. After the experiment, the pharmacist calculates that she has made 12.4 moles of aspirin. What mass of aspirin has the pharmacist made?   (Grade 4-6)

The relative atomic mass, A_r, of C = 12, of H = 1 and of O = 16.

mass = ... g

[Total 2 marks]

4   How many atoms are there in 7 moles of ammonia, NH_3? Give your answer to 3 significant figures.   (Grade 6-7)

.... atoms

[Total 2 marks]

5   A student makes up a volume of a standard solution of copper sulfate with a concentration of 75.0 g dm⁻³. He does this by dissolving powdered copper sulfate in 220 cm³ of water.   (Grade 6-7)

Calculate the mass of copper sulfate that was used to make the solution.

mass = ... g

[Total 1 mark]

6 A student dissolves 56 g of potassium chloride in 400 cm³ of water. (Grade 6-7)

a) Calculate the concentration of the resultant potassium chloride solution in g dm⁻³.

concentration = ... g dm⁻³
[1]

b) The student wants to make a solution with the same concentration using only 300 cm³ of water. Use your answer from part a) to calculate the mass of potassium chloride that the student will need to add to this volume of water to create a solution with the same concentration.

mass = ... g
[1]

[Total 2 marks]

7 A lab technician is making up some solutions for students to use in some of their classes. (Grade 7-9)

a) The technician makes a standard solution of sodium hydroxide for a titration experiment. She makes 600 cm³ of the solution at a concentration of 52 g dm⁻³.

Calculate the number of moles of sodium hydroxide used to make the solution.
Relative formula mass, M_r, of NaOH = 40

number of moles = ...
[2]

b) i) The technician also makes a standard solution of sodium carbonate. The solution has a concentration of 80.0 g dm⁻³ and was made by adding 36.0 g of sodium carbonate to a volume of water. Calculate the volume of water, in cm³, that she used to make the solution.

volume of water = ... cm³
[2]

ii) For a separate experiment, the technician needs a sodium carbonate solution with a concentration of 40.0 g dm⁻³.
What can she do to her 80.0 g dm⁻³ solution to make it this concentration?

....
[1]

[Total 5 marks]

8 A sample of an unknown element contains 1.204×10^{25} atoms. **Grade 7-9**

a) How many moles of atoms of the element are in the sample?

number of moles = ...

[1]

b) Given that the atoms have a mean mass of 9.3×10^{-23} g, what is the identity of the element?

....

[2]

[Total 3 marks]

9 A student is investigating an unidentified acid, which is made up of oxygen, sulfur and hydrogen atoms. **Grade 7-9**

a) Given that 3.5 moles of the acid has a mass of 343 g, what is the relative formula mass of the acid?

relative formula mass = ...

[1]

b) The percentage mass of the acid made up of oxygen atoms is 65%. To the nearest whole number, how many moles of oxygen atoms are in one mole of the acid?

number of moles = ...

[2]

c) In one mole of the acid, there is one mole of sulfur atoms. Deduce the chemical formula of the acid.

chemical formula = ...

[3]

[Total 6 marks]

Topic 1 — Key Concepts in Chemistry

Calculating Empirical Formulas

1 An oxide of lead contains 2.07 g of lead and 0.16 g of oxygen. What is the empirical formula of the lead oxide?

A_r(Pb) = 207, A_r(O) = 16

empirical formula = ...

[Total 2 marks]

2 53.66 g of an oxide of copper contains 10.8 g of oxygen by mass. Calculate the empirical formula of the copper oxide.

A_r(Cu) = 63.5, A_r(O) = 16

empirical formula = ...

[Total 3 marks]

3 83% of the mass of a certain hydrocarbon is made up of carbon atoms. Calculate the empirical formula of the hydrocarbon.

A_r(C) = 12, A_r(H) = 1

empirical formula = ...

[Total 3 marks]

4 A student carried out an experiment to calculate the empirical formula of an oxide of iron. She burnt 3.808 g of iron until it had all reacted. She found that the weight of the product was 5.440 g.

a) Suggest a piece of equipment that the student could use to carry out the reaction in.

....

[1]

b) Calculate the empirical formula of the iron oxide formed during the experiment.
A_r(Fe) = 56, A_r(O) = 16

empirical formula = ...

[3]

[Total 4 marks]

Limiting Reactants

Complete the following sentences by filling in the blanks with the words on the right.

1) If the amount of limiting reactant in a reaction is decreased,
then the amount of product made will ....

not change

2) If the amount of limiting reactant in a reaction is increased,
then the amount of product made will ....

decrease

3) If the amount of an excess reactant is increased,
then the amount of product made will ....

increase

1 James is investigating the reactivity of some metals. As part of his investigation, he places a piece of magnesium metal in a flask containing an excess of hydrochloric acid and monitors the reaction. The reaction produces hydrogen gas and a metal salt solution.

Grade 4-6

a) Which of the reactants is the limiting reactant?

....

[1]

b) James repeats the experiment but changes the starting quantities of magnesium and acid. He lets the reaction proceed to completion, and notes that once the reaction has finished, the reaction vessel contains a small amount of grey metal and a clear solution.

In this second experiment, what is the limiting reactant? Explain your answer.

....

....

....

[2]

[Total 3 marks]

2 An industrial process converts the alkene ethene into ethanol, according to the reaction below.

Grade 6-7

$$C_2H_4 + H_2O \rightarrow CH_3CH_2OH$$

What mass of ethanol can be made from 53 g of ethene, given that water is in excess?

mass = ... g

[Total 2 marks]

3 The following equation shows the complete combustion of ethane in air.

$$2C_2H_6 + 7O_2 \rightarrow 4CO_2 + 6H_2O$$

a) In a complete combustion reaction, some ethane reacted with exactly 128 g of oxygen. Calculate the mass of water produced. Give your answer to three significant figures.

mass = ... g

[3]

b) A company burns ethane to generate power for an industrial process.

As part of a carbon-reducing scheme, the company can only produce a maximum 4.4 tonnes of carbon dioxide per day (where 1 tonne = 1 000 000 g). What is the maximum mass, in tonnes, of ethane that the company can burn each day so as not to exceed the limit of carbon dioxide?

mass = ... tonnes

[3]

[Total 6 marks]

4 Urea, $(NH_2)_2CO$, is a compound that can be synthesised industrially using the following reaction.

$$2NH_3 + CO_2 \rightarrow (NH_2)_2CO + H_2O$$

a) A company makes 120.6 tonnes of urea each day (where 1 tonne = 1 000 000 g). What mass of carbon dioxide, in tonnes, is required to make this mass of urea?

mass = ... tonnes

[3]

b) Usually the reaction happens in an excess of ammonia. However, a leak in a pipe means the mass of ammonia entering the reaction chamber on one day is reduced to 59.5 tonnes.

What is the decrease, in tonnes, in the amount of urea produced on this day?

decrease in mass = ... tonnes

[4]

[Total 7 marks]

Balancing Equations Using Masses

1 Viola reacts 200 g of a metal, **X**, with oxygen. The result of the reaction is 280 g of a single product, which is an oxide of metal **X**.

a) What mass of oxygen was used in the reaction?

mass = ... g

[1]

b) Given that Viola's reaction produced 5 moles of X oxide, write a balanced symbol equation for the reaction of **X** with oxygen.
$A_r(X) = 40$, $A_r(O) = 16$

....

[4]

[Total 5 marks]

2 1.0 g of warm sodium was added to a gas jar containing 1.0 g of chlorine gas (Cl_2). They reacted to form sodium chloride. The equation for the reaction is $2Na + Cl_2 \rightarrow 2NaCl$. Determine which reactant was the **limiting reactant** in this reaction.

$A_r(Na) = 23$, $M_r(Cl_2) = 71$

....

[Total 3 marks]

3 A scientist gently heats tin and iodine together. They react to form a single product, which is a metal halide. Given that 3.57 g of tin reacts exactly with 15.24 g of iodine, write a balanced equation for this reaction.

$A_r(Sn) = 119$, $M_r(I_2) = 254$, $M_r(metal\ halide) = 627$

....

[Total 5 marks]

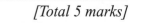

Topic 1 — Key Concepts in Chemistry

States of Matter

Warm-Up

Identify which of the following statements is **false**. Tick **one** box.

Particles in liquids are free to move past each other but tend to stick together. ☐

Particles of a substance in the liquid state have more energy than particles of the same substance in the solid state. ☐

There is hardly any force of attraction between particles in gases. ☐

Particles in liquids are held in fixed positions by strong forces. ☐

1 Substances can exist in three states of matter: solid, liquid or gas. *Grade 4-6*

a) In which of these three states of matter are the forces of attraction between the particles **strongest**?

....
[1]

b) Name the state of matter illustrated in **Figure 1**.

Figure 1

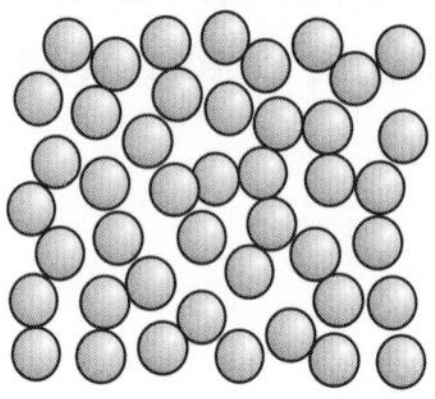

....
[1]

[Total 2 marks]

2 A student has a sample of a solid substance. She heats it gradually until it turns into a liquid. *Grade 6-7*

Describe the differences between the particles in the substance when it is in the liquid state and when it is in the solid state. Give your answer in terms of the movement of the particles and the amount of energy that they have.

....

....

....

....

....

[Total 3 marks]

Changes of State

1   The equations below show four processes that use water as a starting material.

   A: $H_2O_{(l)} \rightarrow H_2O_{(s)}$ **B**: $2H_2O_{(l)} + 2Na_{(s)} \rightarrow 2NaOH_{(aq)} + H_{2(g)}$

   C: $H_2O_{(l)} \rightarrow + H_2O_{(g)}$ **D**: $2H_2O_{(l)} \rightarrow 2H_{2(g)} + O_{2(g)}$

   a) State which equation shows evaporation.

   ....

   [1]

   b) State which **two** equations show chemical changes and explain your answer.

   ....

   ....

   [2]

   [Total 3 marks]

2   **Figure 1** shows some properties of four elements.

Figure 1

Name	Melting point / °C	Boiling point / °C	Appearance		
			solid	liquid	gas
fluorine	−220	−188	colourless	bright yellow	pale yellow
mercury	−39	357	silvery metallic	silvery metallic	n/a
bromine	−7	59	red-brown	red-brown	orange
rubidium	39	688	silvery-white metallic	silvery-white metallic	n/a

During an experiment, samples of each of these four elements were placed in separate test tubes. All four test tubes were then gradually cooled together, from 25 °C to −200 °C.

Describe what you would expect to observe during the experiment as it progressed.
In your answer you should describe what you think will happen to each sample.

....

....

....

....

....

....

....

[Total 4 marks]

           Topic 2 — States of Matter and Mixtures

Purity

1 Misty-Marie is doing a chemistry experiment.
The instructions say she needs to use pure water.
Stanley offers her a bottle labelled '100% Pure Spring Water'.

Grade 4-6

Suggest why Stanley's water is unlikely to be suitable for Misty-Marie's experiment.

....

....

....

....

[Total 2 marks]

2 Copper can be made extremely pure. The melting points of two samples
of copper were measured. Sample **A** had a melting point of 1085 °C
and sample **B** melted over the range 900 – 940 °C.

Grade 4-6

Suggest which of the samples, **A** or **B**, was the **most pure**. Explain your answer.

....

....

....

[Total 2 marks]

3 A scientist is comparing samples of two substances.
One sample is a pure compound, but the other is a mixture.
Both substances are solids at room temperature.

Grade 4-6

a) The scientist decides to work out which is the pure compound by heating both
samples and recording their melting points. Explain how she will be able to tell
which is the pure compound, even if she does not know its melting point.

....

....

....

[2]

b) Suggest what apparatus the scientist could use to
measure the melting points of the substances in the lab.

....

[1]

[Total 3 marks]

Separating Mixtures

1   **Figure 1** shows a set of equipment you could use for separating a mixture in the lab.

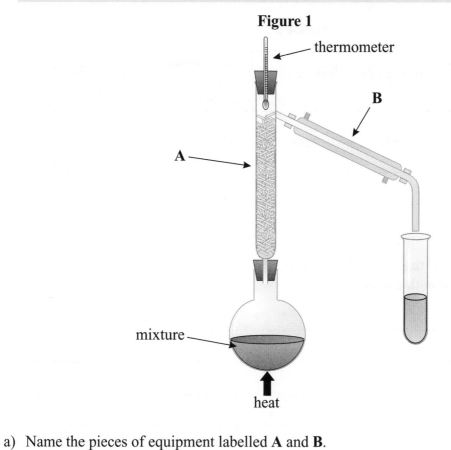

Figure 1

thermometer

B

A

mixture

heat

a)   Name the pieces of equipment labelled **A** and **B**.

i) **A**: ....
    [1]

ii) **B**: ....
    [1]

b) i) What is the name of the separation method this equipment would be used for?

    ....
    [1]

    ii) Describe what type of mixture you would use this method to separate.

    ....

    ....
    [2]

    iii) Reuben is using this method to separate a mixture.
        His mixture contains a substance that is flammable.
        Suggest a suitable piece of equipment that he could use to heat the mixture.

    ....
    [1]
    [Total 6 marks]

2*   A student wants to separate the components of a mixture.
The mixture is a white powder composed of barium sulfate and potassium iodide.
Figure 2 shows some information about the two compounds in the mixture.

Figure 2

Name	Melting point / °C	Boiling point / °C	Appearance at room temperature	Soluble in water?
barium sulfate	1580	1600	white solid	no
potassium iodide	681	1330	white solid	yes

Describe a detailed method that the student could use
to obtain pure samples of **both** compounds.

....

....

....

....

....

....

....

....

....

....

....

....

....

....

....

....

[Total 6 marks]

3 Sodium chloride dissolves in water, but not in ethanol.
Sodium chloride has a melting point of 801 °C and a boiling point of 1413 °C.
Ethanol has a melting point of –114 °C and a boiling point of 78 °C.

a) Suggest a purification method which would separate a mixture of sodium chloride and ethanol, but **not** a mixture of sodium chloride and water. Explain your answer.

....

....

....

....

[3]

b) Suggest a purification method which would separate a mixture of sodium chloride and water and would **also** separate a mixture of sodium chloride and ethanol. Explain your answer.

....

....

....

[2]

[Total 5 marks]

4 **Figure 3** lists the boiling points of three compounds.

Grade 7-9

Figure 3

Name	Formula	Boiling point / °C
cyclopentane	C_5H_{10}	49
cyclohexane	C_6H_{12}	81
ethyl ethanoate	$C_4H_8O_2$	77

Suggest why a mixture of cyclohexane and ethyl ethanoate might be more difficult to separate than a mixture of cyclohexane and cyclopentane.

....

....

....

....

....

[Total 2 marks]

Exam Practice Tip

You might find some of these separation techniques cropping up in questions about other practicals — you often need to use one of them at the end of an experiment to separate out a pure sample of the product from the reaction mixture.

     Topic 2 — States of Matter and Mixtures

Chromatography

1   Olivia analysed an unknown mixture of liquids using paper chromatography.
The solvent she used was ethanol. The chromatogram she produced is shown in **Figure 1**.

Figure 1

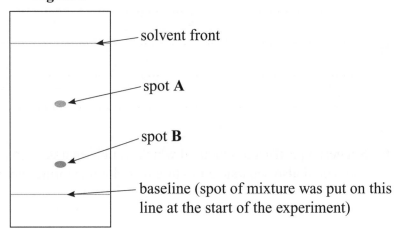

a) Name the mobile phase in Olivia's experiment

....

[1]

b) What does this chromatogram tell you about the number of components in the mixture?
Explain your answer.

....

....

[2]

c) Calculate the R_f value of spot **B**. Use a ruler to help you.

$$R_f = \frac{\text{distance travelled by solute}}{\text{distance travelled by solvent}}$$

$R_f =$ ....

[3]

d) Olivia is given a list of five chemicals.
She is told that her mixture is made up of a combination of some of the chemicals on the list.
Explain how Olivia could use pure samples of the chemicals on the list
to identify the components of the mixture using paper chromatography.

....

....

....

....

[2]

[Total 8 marks]

Topic 2 — States of Matter and Mixtures

2 Lamar wants to analyse the composition of a sample of ink.
The ink is made up of a number of dyes dissolved in a solvent.

Grade 6-7

PRACTICAL

a) The boiling point of the solvent is lower than the boiling point of any of the dyes.

   i) Suggest a method Lamar could use to separate the mixture of dyes from the solvent.

   ....
[1]

   ii) Explain how this method can provide data that could help Lamar to identify the solvent.

   ....

   ....
[1]

b) Lamar uses paper chromatography to analyse the mixtures of dyes in the ink.
He compares the mixture with five different water soluble dyes, A to E.
After 30 minutes, the chromatogram in **Figure 2** was obtained.

Figure 2

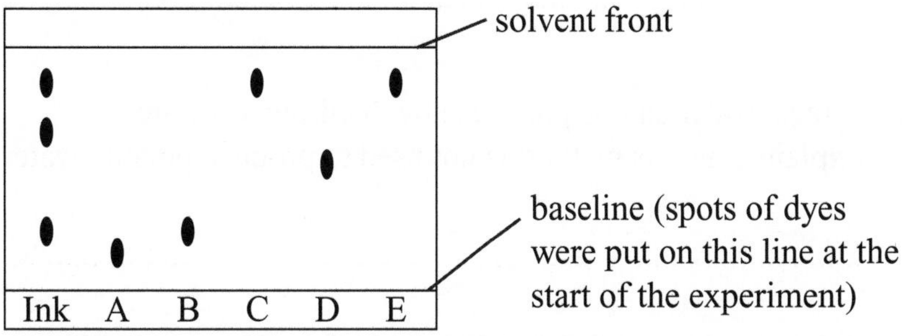

solvent front

baseline (spots of dyes
were put on this line at the
start of the experiment)

Ink A B C D E

Outline the procedure for setting up and running this experiment.

....

....

....

....

....

....
[5]

c) Explain the results shown on Lamar's chromatogram.

....

....

....

....

....

....
[4]

[Total 11 marks]

Topic 2 — States of Matter and Mixtures

Water Treatment

Warm-Up

Tick the boxes to show whether the following statements are **true** or **false**.

	True	False
Potable water is the same as drinking water.	☐	☐
Potable water can only be produced from fresh water found in rivers, streams and reservoirs.	☐	☐
Ordinary tap water can be used in chemical analysis.	☐	☐

1 This question is about potable water. **Grade 4-6**

a) Name **one** source of water used in the production of potable water in the UK.

....

[1]

b) Potable water can be produced by distilling sea water.
Explain why this method is not used to produce potable water in the UK.

....

....

[2]

[Total 3 marks]

2 A purification plant uses multiple steps to purify water. **Grade 6-7**

a) When the water arrives at a water purification plant, it is passed through wire meshes and gravel beds to remove large solid impurities. Give the name of this step.

....

[1]

b) Some water purification plants use aluminium sulfate to carry out a sedimentation step.
How does the aluminium sulfate contribute to the purification process?

....

....

[1]

c) The purification process ends with chlorination.
Describe what happens to the water during this process and state why it is carried out.

....

....

[2]

[Total 4 marks]

Topic 2 — States of Matter and Mixtures

Acids and Bases

Warm-Up

Circle the statements below that are **true**.

As H$^+$ concentration increases, pH decreases.

Acids contain lots of OH$^-$ ions.

Neutral substances have a pH of 8.

Alkalis turn Universal indicator blue/purple.

Acids have pHs of less than 7.

Alkalis are soluble bases.

---

1   This question is about acids and bases.
Figure 1 shows the pH values of some everyday substances.

Figure 1

Substance	pH
Beer	4
Bicarbonate of soda	9
Milk	7

a)   Write the name of the substance in **Figure 1** that is an acid.

....

[1]

b)   What colour would you expect to see if phenolphthalein was added to bicarbonate of soda solution?

....

[1]

c)   Which ion is produced by an acid in aqueous solution? Tick **one** box.

☐   **A** Cl$^-$

☐   **B** H$^+$

☐   **C** OH$^-$

☐   **D** OH$^+$

[1]

[Total 3 marks]

---

2   Which of the following equations shows a neutralisation reaction? Tick **one** box.

☐   **A** $HNO_3 + LiOH \rightarrow LiNO_3 + H_2O$

☐   **B** $Mg + H_2O \rightarrow MgO + H_2$

☐   **C** $Na_2O + H_2O \rightarrow 2NaOH$

☐   **D** $C_4H_{10} + 6\frac{1}{2}O_2 \rightarrow 4CO_2 + 5H_2O$

[Total 1 mark]

3 Acids and bases react together in neutralisation reactions.

Grade 4-6

a) Write the general word equation for a neutralisation reaction between an acid and a base.

....

[1]

b) In terms of hydrogen ions and hydroxide ions, write an ionic equation
for a neutralisation reaction in aqueous solution.

....

[1]

[Total 2 marks]

4 Kevin has samples of three different alkaline solutions. Solution **A** has a pH of 11, solution **B** has a pH of 13 and solution **C** has a pH of 8. State which of Kevin's solutions has the **lowest** concentration of hydroxide ions and explain your answer.

Grade 6-7

....

....

....

[Total 2 marks]

5 Haifa is investigating the properties of a sample of dilute hydrochloric acid, HCl.

Grade 6-7

PRACTICAL

a) She puts 100 cm³ of the acid into a flask.
Suggest a piece of apparatus that Haifa could use to accurately measure out 100 cm³ of the acid.

....

[1]

b) Haifa adds a measured mass of powdered calcium hydroxide to the flask. It reacts completely.
She takes a sample of the resultant solution and tests its pH using universal indicator paper.

i) Suggest what colour the universal indicator paper will turn
when Haifa adds a spot of the solution. Explain your answer.

....

....

[3]

ii) Haifa repeats the same procedure several times. After she adds the fifth lot of calcium hydroxide, she sees a small amount of unreacted solid left at the bottom of the flask.
Suggest what colour the universal indicator paper will turn at this point. Explain your answer.

....

....

[3]

[Total 7 marks]

Topic 3 — Chemical Changes

Strong and Weak Acids

1   Tamal has two beakers, each containing a sample of a different acid.
    The acid in beaker X is **stronger** than the acid in beaker Y.
    The acid in beaker Y is **more concentrated** than the acid in beaker X.

Which row of the table in **Figure 1** could describe the contents of the two beakers? Tick **one** box.

Figure 1

	Beaker X	Beaker Y
☐ **A**	0.002 mol/dm³ HCl	4.0 mol/dm³ CH₃COOH
☐ **B**	4.0 mol/dm³ HCl	0.002 mol/dm³ CH₃COOH
☐ **C**	0.002 mol/dm³ CH₃COOH	4.0 mol/dm³ HCl
☐ **D**	4.0 mol/dm³ CH₃COOH	0.002 mol/dm³ HCl

[Total 1 mark]

2   Methanoic acid, HCOOH, is a **weak acid**.

a) Explain what is meant by the term 'weak acid'.

    ....

    ....
    [1]

b) Write a chemical equation to show how methanoic acid acts as a weak acid.

    ....
    [2]
    [Total 3 marks]

3   Jackie is carrying out an experiment to measure how
    the pH of a strong acid is affected by its concentration.

a) Jackie takes a sample of an acidic solution, A, made by dissolving a solid acid in deionised water.
    He wants to make his sample of the acid more concentrated.
    Which of the following things could he do? Tick **one** box.

    ☐ **A** Add a more dilute solution of the acid to the sample.

    ☐ **B** Add more water to the sample.

    ☐ **C** Add more solution the same as A to the sample.

    ☐ **D** Dissolve more solid acid in the sample.

    [1]

b) At a certain dilution, the hydrogen ion concentration is 0.001 mol/dm³ and the acid has a pH of 3.
    Jackie increases the concentration of hydrogen ions in the sample to 0.1 mol/dm³.
    What is the new pH of the acid?

    ....
    [1]

    [Total 2 marks]

Topic 3 — Chemical Changes

Reactions of Acids

1 June reacts a metal and an acid together in a flask. Which of the following describes the products of this reaction? Tick **one** box.

Grade 4-6

- [ ] **A** A salt and water.
- [ ] **B** A salt and carbon dioxide gas.
- [ ] **C** A salt, water and carbon dioxide gas.
- [ ] **D** A salt and hydrogen gas.

[Total 1 mark]

2 Complete **Figure 1** to show the chemical formulas of the salts created in the reactions involving the following acids.

Grade 6-7

Figure 1

	Hydrochloric acid (HCl)	Nitric acid (HNO_3)	Sulfuric acid (H_2SO_4)
Zinc metal (Zn)	$ZnCl_2$	....	$ZnSO_4$
Calcium carbonate ($CaCO_3$)	$CaCl_2$	$Ca(NO_3)_2$	....
Sodium hydroxide (NaOH)	NaCl	$NaNO_3$	....
Potassium carbonate (K_2CO_3)	....	KNO_3	K_2SO_4

[Total 4 marks]

3 Pauline mixes zinc carbonate, $ZnCO_3$, with hydrochloric acid, HCl, and notes that the mixture starts to bubble as a gas is given off.

Grade 6-7

a) Give the name of the gas that is responsible for the bubbles in the reaction. Describe a test you could perform to identify this gas.

....

....

[3]

b) Write a balanced chemical equation for the reaction between hydrochloric acid and zinc carbonate.

....

[2]

c) What is the name of the salt produced by the reaction?

....

[1]

[Total 6 marks]

Making Insoluble Salts

1 Insoluble salts can be made by precipitation reactions.
Which of the following equations describes a precipitation reaction? Tick **one** box.

Grade 4-6

- [ ] **A** $CuO_{(s)} + 2HCl_{(aq)} \rightarrow CuCl_{2(aq)} + H_2O_{(l)}$
- [ ] **B** $HCl_{(aq)} + NaOH_{(aq)} \rightarrow NaCl_{(aq)} + H_2O_{(l)}$
- [ ] **C** $2HNO_{3(aq)} + ZnCO_{3(s)} \rightarrow Zn(NO_3)_{2(aq)} + H_2O_{(l)} + CO_{2(g)}$
- [ ] **D** $Pb(NO_3)_{2(aq)} + 2NaCl_{(aq)} \rightarrow PbCl_{2(s)} + 2NaNO_{3(aq)}$

[Total 1 mark]

2 Jerry is making a sample of silver chloride, an insoluble salt, by mixing two salt solutions.

Grade 6-7

a) Suggest two salt solutions that Jerry could mix to make silver chloride.

....

....
[1]

b) Once Jerry has made the salt, he pours the whole
solid and salt solution into a filter funnel, as shown in **Figure 1**.

Figure 1

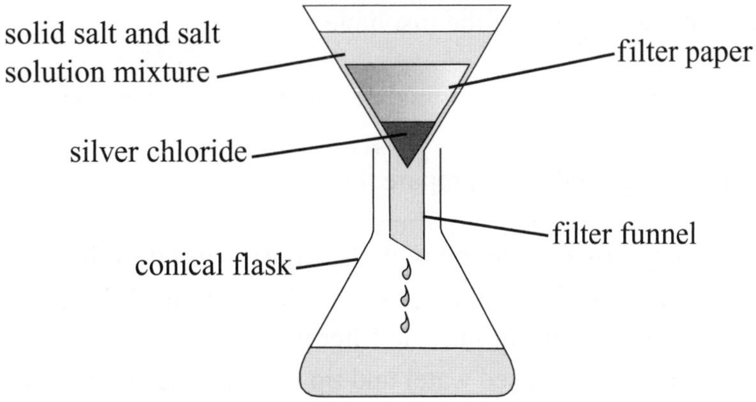

What has Jerry done wrong? Explain how this could affect
the mass of solid salt that he collects from the solution.

....

....

....
[2]

c) After Jerry has isolated the salt, he washes it with deionised water.
Explain why he uses deionised water as opposed to tap water.

....

....
[1]

[Total 4 marks]

Topic 3 — Chemical Changes

42

3 The students in a chemistry class are investigating the properties of calcium salts. (Grade 6-7)

a) They plan to carry out reactions to make calcium nitrate, $Ca(NO_3)_2$, and calcium sulfate, $CaSO_4$. Before they start, four students predict whether the salts will be soluble or insoluble. Which prediction is correct? Tick **one** box.

    ☐ **A** Ashley: "Both calcium salts will be insoluble."

    ☐ **B** Benni: "Both reactions will make soluble calcium salts."

    ☐ **C** Chen: "We'll get an insoluble precipitate of calcium sulfate, but calcium nitrate is soluble in water."

    ☐ **D** Dermot: "Calcium sulfate dissolves in water, but calcium nitrate doesn't, so only calcium nitrate will form as a precipitate."

    [1]

b) In a third reaction, the students want to produce the insoluble salt calcium carbonate, $CaCO_3$. Suggest two soluble salts they could react together to make a precipitate of calcium carbonate.

....

....

[2]

[Total 3 marks]

4 Davina reacts aqueous iron(III) nitrate solution, $Fe(NO_3)_3$, with aqueous sodium hydroxide solution, NaOH, to make an insoluble salt containing iron. (Grade 6-7)

a) Write down the chemical formula of the insoluble salt.

....

[1]

b) Davina used the following method to prepare the salt:

> 1. Mix the sodium hydroxide solution with the iron(III) nitrate solution in a beaker and stir.
> 2. Line a filter funnel with filter paper and place it in a conical flask. Pour the contents of the beaker into the filter paper.
> 3. Rinse the beaker with deionised water and tip this into the filter paper.
> 4. Rinse the contents of the filter paper with deionised water.

  i) Explain why Davina rinsed the beaker and added the rinsings to the filter paper.

  ....

  [1]

  ii) After completing step 4, Davina wants to dry the solid product. Suggest how she could do this.

  ....

  [1]

  iii) Given that Davina used an excess of iron(III) nitrate solution, state which **three** ions will be present in the solution that is left in the conical flask at the end of the experiment.

  ....

  [2]

  [Total 5 marks]

Topic 3 — Chemical Changes   ☹ ☐   ☺ ☐   ☺ ☐

Making Soluble Salts

Nina is making the soluble salt zinc chloride by reacting zinc with hydrochloric acid.
She wants to prepare a pure, dry sample of solid zinc chloride.
The equipment Nina has available is listed below.
Circle the pieces of equipment below that you would expect Nina to use.

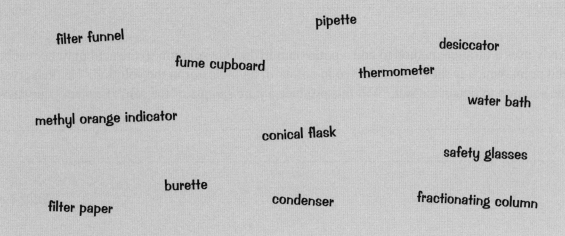

filter funnel

pipette

desiccator

fume cupboard

thermometer

water bath

methyl orange indicator

conical flask

safety glasses

burette

condenser

fractionating column

filter paper

---

1 The following steps are parts of a method you could use to produce
a pure, dry sample of the soluble salt magnesium sulfate, $MgSO_4$,
from solid magnesium hydroxide and sulfuric acid.

1   Slowly heat the solution to evaporate off some of the water.

2   Filter the solid off and dry it in a desiccator.

3   Filter out the excess solid using a filter funnel and filter paper.

4   Add magnesium hydroxide to a flask containing warm sulfuric acid.
Continue adding the magnesium hydroxide until no more reacts
(at this point, the excess solid will just sink to the bottom of the flask).

5   Leave the solution to crystallise.

a) Which is the correct order that these steps should be carried out in? Tick **one** box.

☐ **A** 4, 1, 3, 2, 5

☐ **B** 1, 4, 2, 5, 2

☐ **C** 4, 3, 1, 5, 2

☐ **D** 3, 1, 2, 5, 4

[1]

b) Write a balanced symbol equation, including state symbols, that describes the
reaction between magnesium hydroxide, $Mg(OH)_2$, and sulfuric acid, H_2SO_4.

....

[3]

[Total 4 marks]

44

2 Andy is making a sample of potassium sulfate by reacting potassium hydroxide, KOH, and sulfuric acid, H_2SO_4, together.

Grade 6-7

a) Potassium sulfate is a soluble salt. Explain what is meant by the term soluble in this context.

....

[1]

b) Write a balanced chemical equation for this reaction.

....

[2]

c) Andy uses a titration method to add a potassium hydroxide solution to the acid until he reaches the end point, which is shown by a change in colour of an indicator in the solution. He then crystallises the solution to obtain the salt. Will this produce a pure sample of the salt? Explain your answer.

....

....

[1]

[Total 4 marks]

3 Copper sulfate is a soluble salt that can be made by the reaction between sulfuric acid, H_2SO_4, and copper oxide, CuO.

Grade 7-9

PRACTICAL

a) Write a balanced chemical equation for the reaction between sulfuric acid and copper oxide.

....

[2]

b)* Outline how you could prepare a pure, dry sample of copper sulfate in the lab from sulfuric acid and copper oxide.

....

....

....

....

....

....

....

....

....

....

[6]

[Total 8 marks]

Electrolysis

1 As part of an industrial process, a sample of potassium chloride, KCl, was electrolysed. *(Grade 4-6)*

a) Before the potassium chloride is electrolysed, it either has to be molten or dissolved in solution. Explain why this is necessary.

....

....

[2]

b) During the electrolysis of molten potassium chloride, potassium ions are reduced to potassium metal. At which electrode would you expect this reaction to occur?

....

[1]

[Total 3 marks]

2 Electrolysis is carried out on a solution of copper chloride, $CuCl_2$, using inert electrodes. *(Grade 6-7)*

a) Which of the following ions is **not** present in the solution? Tick **one** box.

☐ **A** H^+ ☐ **B** H_2O^- ☐ **C** Cl^- ☐ **D** Cu^{2+}

[1]

b) What would you expect to see happen at:

i) the anode? ....

ii) the cathode? ....

[2]

[Total 3 marks]

3 A solution of sodium chloride, NaCl, is electrolysed using platinum electrodes. *(Grade 6-7)*

a) Platinum electrodes are an example of inert electrodes.
Explain what is meant by the term 'inert' when referring to electrodes.

....

[1]

b) The sodium chloride solution contains dissolved sodium chloride and water only. List the ions that are present in solution during the electrolysis of sodium chloride solution using inert electrodes.

....

[2]

c) Write balanced half equations to show the reactions that occur at:

i) the anode ....

ii) the cathode ....

[4]

[Total 7 marks]

Topic 3 — Chemical Changes

4 The half-equation for the reaction at the cathode during an electrolysis experiment is $Pb^{2+} + 2e^- \rightarrow Pb$. The half-equation for the reaction at the anode is $2I^- \rightarrow I_2 + 2e^-$.

Grade 6-7

a) Give the definition of the term **electrolyte**.

....

[2]

b) Give the chemical formula of the electrolyte in this experiment,
given that it's a molten ionic compound.

....

[1]

[Total 3 marks]

5* A student is investigating the electrolysis of sodium chloride solution using inert electrodes. Describe how you would set up an electrochemical cell to carry out this investigation and predict what you would observe happening at each electrode as the reaction progressed.

Grade 6-7

....

....

....

....

....

....

....

....

....

[Total 6 marks]

6 When sodium sulfate solution is electrolysed using inert electrodes, sodium is not discharged at the cathode.

Grade 7-9

a) Explain why sodium **is not** discharged at the cathode and state what product **is** discharged instead.

....

....

[3]

b) State which **two** products are discharged at the anode.

....

[2]

c) Suggest an alternative electrolysis experiment that could be
carried out that **would** produce sodium metal at the cathode.

....

[2]

[Total 7 marks]

7   Marco is investigating the electrolysis of copper sulfate. He sets up two cells as shown in **Figure 1**. In cell A, Marco uses platinum electrodes. In cell B, he uses pure copper electrodes. The cells are identical in all other respects.

PRACTICAL

Grade 7-9

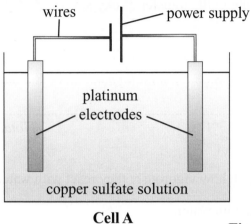

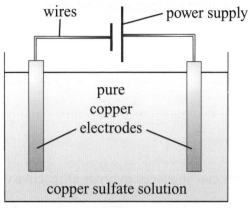

Figure 1

a)   Both cells are turned on and left for 1 hour. Given that the masses of the two cells were the same at the start of the electrolysis, how would you expect them to compare after 1 hour? Explain your answer. Use appropriate half equations to justify your conclusion.

....

....

....

....

....

....

[6]

b)   A similar cell to cell B can be used to purify copper. Give **one** similarity and **one** difference between the cell used to purify copper in industry and cell B.

....

....

[2]

[Total 8 marks]

8   Write half-equations to show what reactions occur at the cathode and the anode when acidified water is electrolysed.

Grade 7-9

Cathode: ....

Anode: ....

[Total 4 marks]

Exam Practice Tip

It's important to remember that when you electrolyse aqueous solutions (rather than molten salts) what products are made will depend on the reactivity of all the ions present in the solution. Make sure you've learnt which ions will be discharged from which solutions. And get plenty of practice at writing half-equations too — they're really important...

Topic 3 — Chemical Changes

Reactivity Series and Reactivity of Metals

1   The reaction that occurs when a metal is burnt in oxygen can be described as an oxidation reaction. Explain why, using ideas about the transfer of oxygen.

Grade 4-6

....

....

....

[Total 2 marks]

2   Metals can be placed in order of reactivity based on how vigorously they react with water.

Grade 4-6

a) Write a word equation for the reaction of sodium with water.

....

[1]

b) Explain, using ideas about oxidation, why iron reacts much more slowly with cold water than sodium does.

....

....

[1]

[Total 2 marks]

3   Some metals can react with water.

Grade 6-7

a) i) Complete the symbol equation below for the reaction of calcium and water. Include state symbols.

$$Ca_{(s)} + 2H_2O_{(l)} \rightarrow \text{.........................} + \text{.........................}$$

[2]

ii) Identify which element is oxidised. Explain your answer in terms of oxygen.

....

....

[2]

iii) Suggest a metal which will react more vigorously with water than calcium. Explain your answer.

....

....

[2]

b) Put the metals sodium, zinc and potassium in order, based on how vigorously you think they would react with water.

Most vigorous .... Least vigorous

[1]

[Total 7 marks]

4 Which of the statements below about metal reactivity is **incorrect**? Tick **one** box. (Grade 6-7)

☐ **A** The easier it is for a metal atom to form a positive ion, the less reactive it will be.

☐ **B** The more resistant a metal atom is to oxidation, the less reactive it will be.

☐ **C** In a reactivity series, you will find a reactive metal above a less reactive metal.

☐ **D** The more reactive a metal is, the faster its reaction with water will be.

[Total 1 mark]

5 Amal performed some experiments to investigate the reactivity of metals. (Grade 6-7)

a) First, Amal placed pieces of four different metals into dilute hydrochloric acid.
Figure 1 shows what the four experiments looked like after 1 minute.

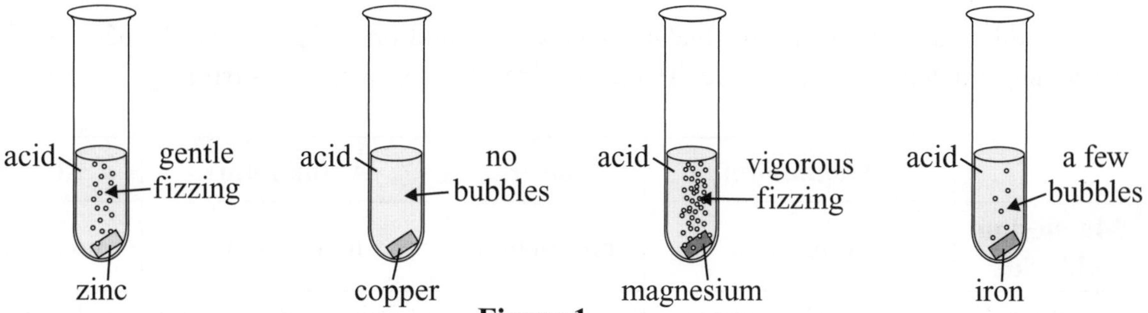

acid — gentle fizzing — zinc   acid — no bubbles — copper   acid — vigorous fizzing — magnesium   acid — a few bubbles — iron

Figure 1

Use **Figure 1** to put these metals in order of reactivity, starting with the **most reactive**.

....

[1]

b) Next, Amal was given samples of three mystery metals, marked **X**, **Y** and **Z**. She put small
pieces of each of the metals in cold water. If there was no reaction with cold water, she
tested the metal to see if it would react with steam. Her results are shown in **Figure 2**.

Metal	Any reaction with cold water?	Any reaction with steam?
X	Reacts vigorously. Hydrogen gas is produced.	
Y	no reaction	Reacts vigorously. Metal is coated with a white solid. Hydrogen gas is produced.
Z	no reaction	no reaction

Figure 2

i) Metal **Y** was zinc. It reacted with the steam to produce hydrogen gas and a white solid.
Name the white solid that was produced by this reaction.

....

[1]

ii) One of the other metals Amal was given was sodium.
Suggest whether sodium was metal **X** or metal **Z**. Give a reason for your answer.

....

....

[1]

[Total 3 marks]

Topic 4 — Extracting Metals and Equilibria

Displacement Reactions

1 A student carries out a displacement reaction by reacting magnesium with an aqueous solution of iron chloride to produce magnesium chloride and iron.

$$Mg_{(s)} + FeCl_{2(aq)} \rightarrow MgCl_{2(aq)} + Fe_{(s)}$$

Explain why this displacement reaction is an example of a redox reaction.

....

....

[Total 2 marks]

2 Shaun adds small pieces of some metals to metal salt solutions. He records whether or not any reaction has taken place. His table of results is shown in **Figure 1**.

	Magnesium	**Silver**	**Aluminium**	**Lead**
Magnesium chloride	no reaction	no reaction	no reaction	no reaction
Silver nitrate	magnesium nitrate and silver formed	no reaction	aluminium nitrate and silver formed	lead nitrate and silver formed
Aluminium chloride	magnesium chloride and aluminium formed	no reaction	no reaction	no reaction
Lead nitrate	magnesium nitrate and lead formed	no reaction	aluminium nitrate and lead formed	no reaction

Figure 1

a) Shaun says "My results show that lead is more reactive than silver."
Do you agree? Explain your answer.

....

....

[1]

b) Construct a balanced symbol equation for the reaction between magnesium and aluminium chloride, $AlCl_3$.

....

[2]

c) Nickel is above lead in the reactivity series. Nickel is a shiny grey metal and nickel nitrate is green in solution. Lead is a dull grey metal and lead nitrate is colourless in solution. Suggest what Shaun would observe if he added nickel to lead nitrate solution.

....

....

....

[2]

[Total 5 marks]

Topic 4 — Extracting Metals and Equilibria

Extracting Metals Using Carbon

1   The method used to extract metals from their ores can be determined using the reactivity series. Part of the reactivity series is shown in **Figure 1**.

Potassium	K	Most Reactive
Calcium	Ca	
Aluminium	Al	
Carbon	C	
Zinc	Zn	
Tin	Sn	
Copper	Cu	Least Reactive

Figure 1

a)   Give the definition of a metal ore.

....

.... *[1]*

b)   Suggest how copper is extracted from its ore in industry.

....

.... *[1]*

c)   State **one** other metal from **Figure 1** that can be extracted in the same way as copper.

.... *[1]*

[Total 3 marks]

2   Iron is extracted from its ore, iron oxide (Fe_2O_3), in a blast furnace using carbon.

a)   Write a balanced equation for this reaction.

.... *[2]*

b)   A certain batch of iron ore that contains impurities of zinc oxide and calcium oxide is reacted in a blast furnace. After the reaction is complete, any metal produced by the reaction was removed. Any unreacted ore was left in the reaction vessel.

The iron metal product was tested for purity and was found to contain traces of another metal. Suggest an identity for the other metal. Explain why it is present.

....

....

....

.... *[3]*

[Total 5 marks]

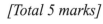

Other Methods of Extracting Metals

1   Aluminium is a metal that is widely used in construction. It can be extracted from its ore, aluminium oxide.   *(Grade 4-6)*

a)   What is the name given to the technique used to extract aluminium from its ore?

....

[1]

b)   As part of the extraction process, aluminium oxide is mixed in cryolite.
What is the purpose of mixing the aluminium oxide with cryolite?

....

[1]

c)   Pure aluminium is more expensive to buy than many metals
which are extracted from their ores by reduction with carbon.
Explain how the extraction process contributes to the higher cost of pure aluminium.

....

....

....

[2]

[Total 4 marks]

2   The increasing demand and the limited supply of metal-rich ores means that scientists are now developing new ways to extract metal from low-grade ores.   *(Grade 6-7)*

a)   Describe how phytoextraction is used to extract some metals from their ores.

....

....

....

....

....

[4]

b)   Give **one** advantage and **one** disadvantage of using phytoextraction to extract metals from their ores.

....

....

....

[2]

c)   Name one other biological method of extracting metals from low-grade ores.

....

[1]

[Total 7 marks]

Topic 4 — Extracting Metals and Equilibria

Recycling

1 This question is on recycling. (Grade 6-7)

a) An alternative to recycling is disposing of waste into landfill.
Give **one** disadvantage associated with using landfill to dispose of waste.

....

[1]

b) Avoiding using landfill is one environmental advantage of recycling. Give **two** other environmental reasons why recycling is considered more sustainable than making new materials.

....

....

[2]

c) Give **two** economic benefits of recycling.

....

....

[2]

[Total 5 marks]

2 Rachel is sorting some rubbish that has accumulated around her house. (Grade 6-7)

a) Rachel has three pieces of rubbish made from three different materials, **A**, **B** and **C**.
Some data about the materials is shown in **Figure 1**.

Material	Availability of resource	Energy to recycle	Energy to extract
A	Abundant	High	Low
B	Limited	Low	High
C	Limited	Medium	High

Figure 1

From the data given, which material in **Figure 1** is the **best** to recycle? Explain your answer.

....

....

....

....

[2]

b) Rachel is able to recycle plastic bottles at her local recycling centre.
Given that many parts of the manufacturing process involve using fractions of crude oil, explain why it is important to recycle plastics.

....

....

[1]

[Total 3 marks]

Topic 4 — Extracting Metals and Equilibria

Life Cycle Assessments

A company is developing a new product. Identify the factors that they should consider when producing a life cycle assessment. Tick **two** boxes.

Colour of the product ☐   Demand for the product ☐

Recyclability of the product ☐   Attractiveness of the product ☐

Source of raw materials ☐   Profitability of the product ☐

1   A furniture company is designing a new range of chairs for children.
They need to decide whether the chairs will be made out of polypropene or timber.   Grade 6-7

a)   The company carries out a life cycle assessment of both possible products.
Describe the purpose of a life cycle assessment.

....

....
[1]

b)   Some data about the two materials are shown in **Figure 1**.

Material	Source	Relative Energy Cost to Make/Extract	Cost
Timber	Trees	1	Medium
Poly(propene)	Crude oil	15	Low

Figure 1

Use the data in **Figure 1** to explain which material would be the **best** choice
to make the chairs from, in terms of sustainability. Explain your answer.

....

....

....

....

....
[3]

c)   Suggest **two** factors, other than those given in **Figure 1**, that the company should consider in their
life cycle assessment when deciding whether to make the chairs from timber or polypropene.

....

....
[2]

[Total 6 marks]

2 A garden tool company is considering the environmental costs of producing a rake.

Grade
6-7

a) The rake contains components made from iron.
Suggest **two** environmental problems associated with extracting iron from its ore.

....

....

[2]

b) The rake contains parts that cannot be recycled, so the company thinks
that it is likely to be disposed of in landfill at the end of its life span.
Give **one** disadvantage of disposing of waste using landfill.

....

[1]

c) The rake is sold in plastic packaging.
Suggest a sustainable way that consumers could dispose of the packaging.

....

[1]

[Total 4 marks]

3 A toy company is carrying out a life cycle assessment of four prototype toys.
Figure 2 displays some of the data from their assessments.

Grade
7-9

Toy	CO_2 emissions (kg)	Solvent use (dm³)	Energy consumption (MJ)
A	16.2	3981	267.84
B	14.8	2672	212.26
C	14.9	3876	159.82
D	12.4	2112	174.56

Figure 2

Using the data in the table, evaluate the relative environmental impact of producing each toy.

....

....

....

....

....

....

....

[Total 4 marks]

Exam Practice Tip

You may be given data and asked to figure out which product has the biggest or smallest environmental impact. It's likely that there won't be an obvious answer at first glance — some products may have really low CO_2 emissions but may pollute lots of water. You'll have to look at <u>all</u> the factors and decide which product is the best or worst overall.

Topic 4 — Extracting Metals and Equilibria

Dynamic Equilibrium

Complete the paragraph below by circling the correct option from the choices.

The Haber Process is <u>an irreversible / a reversible</u> reaction that forms <u>ammonia / sulfuric acid</u> from hydrogen and nitrogen. The nitrogen used in the process is extracted from <u>the air / crude oil</u> and the hydrogen is extracted from <u>the air / natural gas</u>.

The conditions used for the Haber Process are a temperature of <u>200 °C / 450 °C</u>, a pressure of <u>250 atm / 200 atm</u> and in the presence of an <u>iron / aluminium</u> catalyst.

1 Dynamic equilibrium can only be achieved in reversible reactions. *(Grade 4-6)*

a) Compare the rates of the forwards and backwards reactions at dynamic equilibrium. State how this affects the concentrations of reactants and products present at dynamic equilibrium.

....

....

[2]

b) Dynamic equilibrium can only be reached in a closed system. Explain what is meant by a 'closed system'.

....

....

[1]

c) During a certain reversible reaction, the equilibrium lies to the left. How should the concentration of the reactants be altered in order to increase the rate of product formation?

....

[1]

[Total 4 marks]

2 An aqueous solution of blue copper(II) ions can react with chloride ions to form a yellow copper compound. The ionic equation for this reaction is: $Cu^{2+} + 4Cl^- \rightleftharpoons [CuCl_4]^{2-}$ *(Grade 6-7)*

a) What does the symbol '$\rightleftharpoons$' mean in this reaction?

....

[1]

b) A solution containing copper(II) ions is mixed with a solution containing chloride ions in a flask. The solution quickly turns green. When observed for a few minutes no further change in colour can be seen. Explain these observations.

....

....

....

[2]

[Total 3 marks]

Le Chatelier's Principle

1   The equilibrium position of a reaction is dependent on
the conditions that the reaction is carried out under.
(Grade 4-6)

a) What does Le Chatelier's Principle say about the effect of changing
the conditions of a reversible reaction at equilibrium?

....

[1]

b) State **two** conditions you could change in order to alter the
position of equilibrium of a reaction that happens in solution.

....

....

[2]

[Total 3 marks]

2   Methanol can be manufactured industrially from a gas mixture of carbon monoxide
and hydrogen in the following reaction: $CO_{(g)} + 2H_{2(g)} \rightleftharpoons CH_3OH_{(g)}$.
This occurs over a Cu-ZnO-Al$_2$O$_3$ catalyst, under conditions of 250 °C and 50 –100 atm.
The forward reaction is exothermic.
(Grade 6-7)

a) Under a certain set of conditions, the equilibrium lies to the right.
Describe what this means, in terms of the concentration of products and reactants.

....

....

[1]

b) Identify which of the following statements is **false**. Tick **one** box.

☐   **A** A decrease in the concentration of CO shifts the position of equilibrium to the left.

☐   **B** Increasing the concentration of H$_2$ shifts the position of equilibrium to the right.

☐   **C** Increasing the temperature to 470 °C shifts the position of equilibrium to the left.

☐   **D** The Cu-ZnO-Al$_2$O$_3$ catalyst shifts the position of equilibrium to the right.

[1]

c) Amara says, to increase the yield of the reaction, they should decrease the pressure of
the reaction. Russell disagrees. Which student do you agree with? Explain your answer.

....

....

....

....

[2]

[Total 4 marks]

Topic 4 — Extracting Metals and Equilibria

3 A mixture of iodine monochloride (ICl) and chlorine is sealed in a gas syringe. The gases react in a reversible reaction to form iodine trichloride (ICl_3) and eventually reach an equilibrium. The equation for the reaction is: $ICl_{(g)} + Cl_{2(g)} \rightleftharpoons ICl_{3(s)}$.

Grade 7-9

a) Given that the forward reaction is exothermic, explain how the relative quantities of ICl and ICl_3 would change if the mixture was heated, and all other conditions remained the same.

....

....

....

[2]

b) Explain how the relative quantities of ICl and ICl_3 would change if the plunger were pushed into the syringe, and the temperature remained constant.

....

....

....

[3]

[Total 5 marks]

4 Dinitrogen tetroxide (N_2O_4) is a colourless gas. It decomposes in a reversible reaction to form the brown gas, nitrogen dioxide (NO_2). The reaction equation is: $N_2O_{4(g)} \rightleftharpoons 2NO_{2(g)}$.

Grade 7-9

a) When a sample of N_2O_4 is left to decompose in a sealed tube, a pale brown colour can be seen. If this mixture is heated, the colour becomes a darker brown. Explain this observation and predict whether the forward reaction is exothermic or endothermic.

....

....

....

[3]

b) Explain how you would expect the colour of the equilibrium mixture to change if the pressure of the mixture is decreased, and all other conditions are kept the same.

....

....

....

....

[3]

[Total 6 marks]

Exam Practice Tip

Working out what happens to the position of an equilibrium when you change the conditions can be a bit of a brain twister. Just remember that for any change that's made, the reaction will try to do the opposite. So if you increase the temperature the endothermic reaction will speed up, if you increase the pressure the equilibrium will move to the side where there are fewer moles of gas, and if you increase the concentration of a reactant you'll get more products.

Topic 4 — Extracting Metals and Equilibria

Transition Metals

Warm-Up

Circle all of the elements listed below that are transition metals.
(Use a periodic table to help if you need it.)

nickel   magnesium   sulfur   chromium   tin   iodine

calcium   potassium   titanium   aluminium   cobalt   silver   silicon

1 Four examples of the uses of transition metals and their compounds
are listed below. For each example, give **one** common property
of transition metals that makes the material suitable for that use.

Grade
4-6

a) Tantalum is used to make parts for high-temperature furnaces.

....

[1]

b) Tungsten can be used to make weights for fishing hooks.

....

[1]

c) Oxides of iron can be used to make stained glass for windows.

....

[1]

d) Copper can be used to make pipes to carry water.

....

[1]

[Total 4 marks]

2 Vanadium is a transition metal with atomic number 23.
Several different oxides of vanadium exist, for example VO_2 and V_2O_5.

Grade
6-7

a) The Contact Process is used to produce sulfuric acid from sulfur, oxygen and water.
Vanadium pentoxide, V_2O_5, is added to the reaction vessel during the process. This increases
the rate of the reaction. Suggest what role vanadium pentoxide is playing in this process.

....

[1]

b) Carys has samples of vanadium(IV) oxide, VO_2, and sodium oxide, Na_2O.
One sample is a deep blue powder and the other is a white powder.
Which one would you expect to be the vanadium(IV) oxide? Explain your answer.

....

....

[1]

[Total 2 marks]

Alloys

1 Metals are able to be bent and shaped. **Grade 6-7**

   a) Explain how the structure and bonding in metals means they are able to be bent and shaped.

   ....

   ....
   [2]

   b) An alloy is a mixture of a metal and at least one other element.
   Explain why it is usually harder to change the shape of an alloy than a pure metal.

   ....

   ....

   ....

   ....
   [3]

   [Total 5 marks]

2 This question is about different alloys and their uses. **Grade 6-7**
   Figure 1 shows some data about the properties of four alloys.

Figure 1

Alloy	Carbon Composition (%)	Strength (MPa)	Density (g cm⁻³)
Alloy 1 (stainless steel)	0.07	200	8.1
Alloy 2 (low carbon steel)	0.1	250	7.6
Alloy 3 (high carbon steel)	1.6	350	7.9
Alloy 4 (aluminium alloy)	0	115	2.6

   a) Use the data in **Figure 1** to state the effect on strength of increasing the carbon content in steel.

   ....
   [1]

   b) A vice is used to hold an object in place while work is carried out on it.
   The material a vice is made from needs to be strong and heavy to hold objects in place.
   Suggest which alloy, from **Figure 1**, would be the **most suitable** for this purpose.

   ....
   [1]

   c) Alloy 4 has the lowest strength value of all the metals shown in the table and yet it is used
   to make many parts of commercial aircraft. Using the data in **Figure 1**, explain why this is.

   ....
   [1]

   [Total 3 marks]

Corrosion

1 Electroplating is a method used to coat a metal object with another metal using electrolysis. *Grade 4-6*

Give **two** reasons why objects are electroplated.

....

....

[Total 2 marks]

2 Martha and Joe both own bikes with iron bike chains. Martha leaves her bike outside and, after a week, discovers that the chain has started to rust. *Grade 6-7*

a) Joe keeps his bike inside. Is his bike more or less likely to rust than Martha's? Explain your answer.

....

....

[2]

b) Martha buys a new iron bike chain. She decides to oil the chain to prevent it from rusting. Explain why oiling is a suitable method for protecting a bike chain from rusting.

....

....

[2]

[Total 4 marks]

3 There are several methods that can be used to prevent the corrosion of metals and alloys. *Grade 6-7*

a) A ship manufacturer wants to prevent the corrosion of a steel ship using sacrificial protection. Describe what is meant by sacrificial protection and explain how it protects the ship.

....

....

....

....

[3]

b) A roofing company coats an iron roof with a layer of zinc to protect it from rusting. After a while, the zinc layer becomes scratched. Would you expect the iron roofing to begin to rust? Explain your answer.

....

....

[2]

[Total 5 marks]

Topic 5 — Separate Chemistry 1

Titrations

1   A student carried out a titration where 0.165 mol dm⁻³ hydrochloric acid was used to neutralise 22.0 cm³ of magnesium hydroxide solution. He repeated the titration three times.

a) Calculate the mean titre of hydrochloric acid using the results in **Figure 1**.
    Ignore any anomalous results.

	Titration			
	1	2	3	4
Titre (cm³)	35.10	33.30	33.40	33.35

Figure 1

Mean = ... cm³

[2]

b) Using your result from part a), calculate the number of moles of hydrochloric acid that were needed to neutralise the solution of magnesium hydroxide. Give your answer to 3 significant figures.

Moles = ... mol

[2]

[Total 4 marks]

2   Annalise carried out four repeats of a titration. She calculated the mean titre and found that 40.0 cm³ of 0.100 mol dm⁻³ sodium hydroxide was used to neutralise 20.0 cm³ of hydrochloric acid. The equation for the reaction is: NaOH + HCl → NaCl + H₂O

a) Calculate the concentration of the hydrochloric acid in mol dm⁻³.

Concentration = ... mol dm⁻³

[3]

b) Convert the concentration of the hydrochloric acid to g dm⁻³.
    (Relative atomic masses: H = 1, Cl = 35.5)

Concentration = ... g dm⁻³

[2]

[Total 5 marks]

3 A chemist completes a titration where 0.00850 moles of potassium hydroxide are neutralised by 0.0250 dm³ of sulfuric acid. The equation for the reaction is:

$$2KOH + H_2SO_4 \rightarrow K_2SO_4 + 2H_2O$$

What is the concentration of the sulfuric acid in g dm⁻³? (Relative formula mass of $H_2SO_4 = 98$)

....

....

....

....

[Total 3 marks]

4 Amy has a sodium hydroxide solution of an unknown concentration. She plans to find the concentration of the solution by titrating it with a 0.200 mol dm⁻³ solution of sulfuric acid.

Grade 7-9   **PRACTICAL**

a)* Describe how to carry out a titration, with reference to the equipment used.

....

....

....

....

....

....

....

....

....

....

....

[6]

b) It took 22.5 cm³ of the 0.200 mol dm⁻³ solution of sulfuric acid to neutralise 25.0 cm³ of sodium hydroxide solution. The equation for the reaction is: $2NaOH + H_2SO_4 \rightarrow Na_2SO_4 + 2H_2O$
Calculate the concentration of the sodium hydroxide. Give your answer to 3 significant figures.

Concentration = ... mol dm⁻³

[4]

[Total 10 marks]

Topic 5 — Separate Chemistry 1

Percentage Yield

1 Kezia and Steven are reacting some lithium with water to form lithium hydroxide and hydrogen gas. From the mass of reactants, they calculate the theoretical yield of lithium hydroxide to be 25 g.

Grade 4-6

a) Kezia finds that 17 g of lithium hydroxide is produced.
   What is the percentage yield of lithium hydroxide? Tick **one** box.

   ☐ **A** 63%

   ☐ **B** 72%

   ☐ **C** 68%

   ☐ **D** 54%

   [1]

b) Steven's experiment produces 22 g of lithium hydroxide.
   Calculate the percentage yield of lithium hydroxide in his reaction.

   Percentage yield = ... %
   [3]
   [Total 4 marks]

2 In a precipitation reaction, copper sulfate solution reacts with sodium hydroxide solution. The equation for the reaction is:
$$CuSO_4 + 2NaOH \rightarrow Cu(OH)_2 + Na_2SO_4$$

Grade 6-7

a) If 39.75 g of copper sulfate reacts with an excess of sodium hydroxide, calculate the theoretical yield of the copper hydroxide. Give your answer to 3 significant figures.
   (Relative atomic masses: $Cu = 63.5$, $S = 32$, $O = 16$, $H = 1$)

   Theoretical yield = ... g
   [3]

b) A student carries out this reaction and produces 16.5 g of copper hydroxide. Use your answer in part a) to calculate the percentage yield of the reaction to 3 significant figures.

   Percentage yield = ... %
   [3]
   [Total 6 marks]

3 When heated, calcium carbonate decomposes to form calcium oxide and carbon dioxide.
The equation for the reaction is: $CaCO_3 \rightarrow CaO + CO_2$

In an industrial reaction, 68.00 kg of calcium carbonate decomposed to form
28.56 kg of calcium oxide, CaO. Calculate the percentage yield of calcium oxide.
(Relative atomic masses: Ca = 40, C = 12, O = 16)

Percentage yield = ... %

[Total 6 marks]

4 Ammonia is produced in the Haber process by reacting nitrogen gas with hydrogen gas.
The equation for this reaction is: $N_2 + 3H_2 \rightleftharpoons 2NH_3$

a) A factory used 14 kg of nitrogen gas to produce 4.5 kg of ammonia.
Calculate the percentage yield for the reaction.
(Relative atomic masses: N = 14, H = 1)

Percentage yield = ... %

[6]

b) Suggest **two** reasons why the percentage yield was less than 100%.

....

....

[2]

c) Give **two** reasons why it is desirable for a factory to obtain as high a percentage yield as possible.

....

....

[2]

[Total 10 marks]

Exam Practice Tip

Don't forget that percentage yield is just one factor that businesses consider when they're choosing a process to make chemicals in industry. You might get an exam question where you have to think about why a company might use a reaction to make a chemical by thinking about factors like atom economy and rate of reaction as well as percentage yield.

Topic 5 — Separate Chemistry 1

Atom Economy

Warm-Up

Complete the table by calculating the atom economy for the two reactions.

Reaction	M_r of desired product	Total M_r of all products	Atom Economy (%)
$NaOH + HCl \rightarrow NaCl + H_2O$	58.5	76.5	....
$2Cu + O_2 \rightarrow 2CuO$	159	159	....

1   Some chemicals can be made by several different reactions. Industrial companies need to take different factors into consideration before deciding which reaction pathway is the most profitable and environmentally friendly. **Figure 1** shows data for three different reactions that each produce the same desired product.

Figure 1

Reaction	Atom economy (%)	Percentage yield (%)	Rate	Any useful by-products?
A	100	84	Medium	N/A (no by-products)
B	?	64	Slow	Yes
C	73.5	53	Fast	No

a) i) Give the definition of atom economy.

....

....

[1]

ii) In reaction **B**, the relative formula mass of all the products is 141 and the relative formula mass of the desired product is 111. Use this data to calculate the atom economy of the reaction. Give your answer to 3 significant figures.

Atom economy = ... %

[3]

b) Use the table and your answer to part a) ii) to suggest which reaction pathway would be the most suitable to be carried out in industry. Explain your answer.

....

....

....

....

....

[3]

[Total 7 marks]

2 Magnesium chloride has a variety of applications, including use in fertilisers, waste water treatment and medicine. It can be produced by several different reactions. Three reactions are shown below.

X $Mg + 2HCl \rightarrow MgCl_2 + H_2$
Y $MgCO_3 + 2HCl \rightarrow MgCl_2 + H_2O + CO_2$
Z $MgO + 2HCl \rightarrow MgCl_2 + H_2O$

(Relative atomic masses: Mg = 24, Cl = 35.5, O = 16, C = 12, H = 1)

a) i) Calculate the relative molecular mass of magnesium chloride.

relative molecular mass = ...
[1]

ii) Calculate the atom economy reaction X. Give your answer to 2 significant figures.

Atom economy = ... %
[4]

iii)Calculate the atom economy reaction Y. Give your answer to 2 significant figures.

Atom economy = ... %
[4]

iv)Calculate the atom economy reaction Z. Give your answer to 2 significant figures.

Atom economy = ... %
[4]

b) A company is looking at the cost implications of using each of the reactions. Explain how the atom economy of a reaction can affect:

i) the amount of raw materials needed to make a certain amount of product.

....

....
[1]

ii) the cost associated with disposing of chemical waste.

....

....
[2]

c) Using your answers to part a), suggest which of the three reactions, **X**, **Y** or **Z**, would be the **least** profitable method for making magnesium chloride in industry.

....
[1]

[Total 17 marks]

Topic 5 — Separate Chemistry 1

The Haber Process

1 The Haber process uses the following exothermic reaction: $N_{2(g)} + 3H_{2(g)} \rightleftharpoons 2NH_{3(g)}$ **Grade 4-6**
The conditions used for the reaction affect how quickly it reaches equilibrium.

In terms of how quickly equilibrium is reached, what is the effect of:

a) increasing the pressure? ....

[1]

b) decreasing the temperature? ....

[1]

[Total 2 marks]

2 The Haber process makes ammonia, NH_3, in an exothermic reaction between hydrogen and   **Grade 7-9**
nitrogen. The reaction is carried out at a pressure of 200 atm and a temperature of 450 °C.

a) i) A company increases the temperature in the reaction vessel for the Haber process to 580 °C.
Which of the following is the result of this change in temperature? Tick **one** box.

☐ **A** Higher rate of reaction.

☐ **B** Lower rate of reaction.

☐ **C** No change in the rate of reaction.

☐ **D** Rate of reaction is halved.

[1]

ii) The company thinks the increase in temperature will increase the yield of product from the
Haber process. Do you agree or disagree with the company? Explain your answer.

....

....

....

[2]

b) In a bid to make the process cheaper, the company decides
to reduce the pressure at which they carry out the Haber process.
Give **two** disadvantages of using a low pressure to carry out the Haber process.

....

....

[2]

c) The Haber process uses an iron catalyst. How does the iron catalyst affect:

i) the rate of the reaction? ....

[1]

ii) the yield? ....

[1]

[Total 7 marks]

Topic 5 — Separate Chemistry 1

Fertilisers

Use the words below to complete the sentences about fertilisers.
You don't have to use every word, but each word can only be used once.

| nitrogen | hydrogen | ammonium | potassium | phosphorus | nitric acid |

Fertilisers are made from compounds containing the elements nitrogen, ...

and .... , which are essential for plant growth. The salt ....

nitrate is a fertiliser which can be made by reacting ammonia with ....

1   A student is making a sample of ammonium sulfate crystals using a titration method.
She adds an indicator to dilute sulfuric acid, then adds ammonia until she sees a colour change.
The student then crystallises the solution and is left with impure ammonium sulfate crystals.

Grade 6-7

a) i) Suggest a piece of equipment that she could use to add the ammonia solution to the acid.

....

[1]

ii) Suggest an indicator that she could use to show when the reaction is complete.

....

[1]

b) What should the student have done to produce pure ammonium sulfate crystals?

....

....

....

[2]

c) In industry, the same reaction is used to make ammonium sulfate, but the method is different.
Give **one** reason why factories do **not** use this laboratory method to produce ammonium sulfate.

....

....

[1]

[Total 5 marks]

2   The Haber process is used to produce ammonia.
It is said that without the Haber process, it would be impossible to grow
enough food to feed the population of the world. Suggest why this is true.

Grade 7-9

....

....

....

[Total 3 marks]

Calculations with Gases

For the questions on these pages, you may need the following information:
One mole of any gas occupies 24 dm³ at room temperature and pressure.

1   Hydrogen, H_2, and sulfur dioxide, SO_2, are both gases at room temperature and pressure.

a) Calculate the volume of 23.0 moles of H_2 at room temperature and pressure.

Volume = ... dm³
[1]

b) Calculate the volume of 96 g of SO_2, at room temperature and pressure.
(Relative formula mass of SO_2 = 64)

Volume = ... dm³
[2]

[Total 3 marks]

2   A student burned 7.5 g of ethane, C_2H_6, in an excess of oxygen.
The reaction produced water and carbon dioxide.
$$C_2H_{6(g)} + 3\tfrac{1}{2}O_{2(g)} \rightarrow 2CO_{2(g)} + 3H_2O_{(l)}$$

a) Calculate the volume of ethane used in the reaction, at room temperature and pressure.
(Relative atomic masses: C = 12, H = 1, O = 16)

Volume = ... dm³
[3]

b) Using the reaction equation and the amount of ethane burned,
calculate the volume of CO_2 produced at room temperature and pressure.

Volume = ... dm³
[2]

[Total 5 marks]

3 A student took some calcium carbonate, in the form of marble chips, and added hydrochloric acid. The equation for the reaction is:

$$CaCO_{3(s)} + 2HCl_{(aq)} \rightarrow CaCl_{2(aq)} + CO_{2(g)} + H_2O_{(l)}$$

a) 920 cm³ of carbon dioxide, CO_2, was produced during the reaction.
This had a mass of 1.76 g. Calculate the molar volume of the carbon dioxide.
(Relative atomic masses: C = 12, O = 16)

Molar volume = ... dm³ mol⁻¹
[2]

b) The student repeated the experiment under a different set of conditions.
This time, 175 cm³ of carbon dioxide with a molar volume of 25.0 dm³ mol⁻¹ was produced.
Calculate the mass of carbon dioxide produced in this reaction.

Mass = ... g
[2]

[Total 4 marks]

4 Carbon dioxide can be produced by reacting oxygen with carbon monoxide.

$$2CO_{(g)} + O_{2(g)} \rightarrow 2CO_{2(g)}$$

a) A student reacted 28 g of carbon monoxide with oxygen at room temperature and pressure.
Calculate the volume of oxygen involved in the reaction.
(Relative atomic masses: C = 12, O = 16)

Volume of oxygen = ... dm³
[4]

b) Calculate the volume of carbon dioxide produced in the reaction in part a).

Volume of carbon dioxide = ... dm³
[1]

[Total 5 marks]

       Topic 5 — Separate Chemistry 1

Fuel Cells

1 Fuel cells are an alternative way of producing energy, instead of burning crude oil. ⟨Grade 4-6⟩

a) Give the definition of a fuel cell.

....

....
[2]

b) Which of the following statements about fuel cells is **correct**? Tick **one** box.

☐ **A** Fuel cells produce a voltage indefinitely.

☐ **B** Fuel cells produce a voltage until one of the reactants is completely used up.

☐ **C** Fuel cells start to produce a voltage once all the reactants are used up.

☐ **D** Fuel cells produce a voltage until the reactants are partly used up.

[1]

[Total 3 marks]

2 Most cars on the road today are powered by internal combustion engines. Hydrogen-oxygen fuel cells could replace internal combustion engines in the future. ⟨Grade 6-7⟩

a) Explain why hydrogen-oxygen fuel cells are considered 'cleaner' than internal combustion engines.

....

....

....
[2]

b) Explain why using hydrogen as a fuel instead of petrol might still require the use of fossil fuels.

....

....

....
[2]

c) Give **one** other disadvantage of using hydrogen-oxygen fuel cells to power cars.

....

....
[1]

[Total 5 marks]

Exam Practice Tip

You might get an exam question about the advantages and disadvantages of using fuel cells for a particular purpose. Make sure you think carefully about your answer — some advantages and disadvantages only apply to certain uses.

Topic 5 — Separate Chemistry 1

Group 1 — Alkali Metals

1 The alkali metals are found in Group 1 of the periodic table. (Grade 4-6)

a) Which of the following statements is the **best** description of the alkali metals? Tick **one** box.

☐ **A** Soft metals with relatively high melting points.

☐ **B** Soft metals with relatively low melting points.

☐ **C** Hard metals with relatively high melting points.

☐ **D** Hard metals with relatively low melting points.

[1]

b) The alkali metals readily react to form ionic compounds.
Explain why their ions usually have a charge of +1.

....

....

[2]

[Total 3 marks]

2 A teacher is demonstrating the reactions between water and some alkali metals to her class. In one reaction, she adds a small piece of potassium to cold water. (Grade 6-7)

a) Name the **two** products of this reaction.

....

[2]

b) Describe what you would expect to see if a small piece of potassium was added to cold water.

....

....

....

....

[2]

c) It is **not** safe to carry out the reaction between rubidium and water in the laboratory.
Explain why this is the case, using ideas about the electronic configurations of Group 1 metals.

....

....

....

....

....

[3]

[Total 7 marks]

Group 7 — Halogens

Which of the following statements about the halogens is **true**? Tick **one** box.

☐ They are non-metals that exist as single atoms.

☐ They are metals that exist as single atoms.

☐ They are non-metals that exist as molecules of two atoms.

☐ They are metals that exist as molecules of two atoms.

1 Amelia is testing gases. (Grade 4-6)

Figure 1 shows a gas being tested.

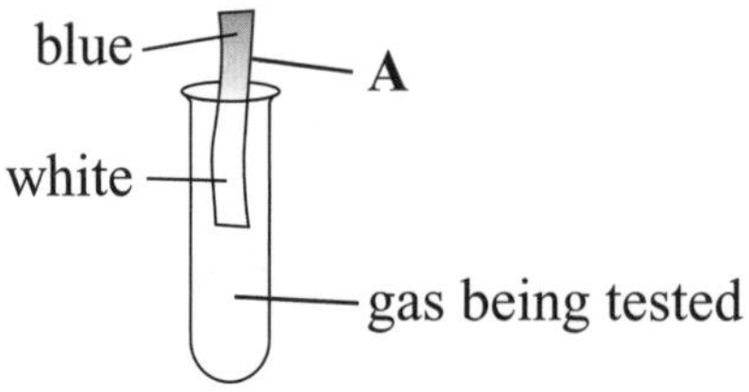

Figure 1

a) Identify the item labelled **A** in **Figure 1**.

....

[1]

b) Suggest which gas was present in the test tube.

....

[1]

[Total 2 marks]

2 The halogens can react with alkali metals to form metal halide salts. (Grade 4-6)

a) Name the metal halide salt that will be formed when the following pairs of elements react.

i) Bromine and sodium.

....

[1]

ii) Iodine and potassium.

....

[1]

b) When chlorine gas reacts with lithium, the salt lithium chloride, LiCl, is formed.
Write the balanced symbol equation for this reaction.

....

[2]

[Total 4 marks]

3 A chemist is carrying out some reactions involving halogens. **Grade 6-7**

a) i) In his first experiment he reacts hydrogen gas with chlorine gas.
Write a balanced chemical equation for this reaction.

....

[2]

ii) The chemist dissolves the product of this reaction in water and adds universal indicator.
What colour will the solution turn? Explain your answer.

....

....

[2]

b) The chemist carries out another reaction at room temperature and pressure, using a different gaseous halogen. Determine which of the halogens he must be using. Explain your answer.

....

....

[2]

c) Describe the appearance of bromine at room temperature.

....

[2]

[Total 8 marks]

4 The reactivity of halogens is dependent on their electronic configuration. **Grade 7-9**

a) Describe the electronic configuration of the halogens and how it changes down Group 7.

....

....

....

[2]

b) Sodium reacts violently with fluorine, at room temperature, to form sodium fluoride.
Predict how astatine might react with sodium at room temperature. Explain your answer.

....

....

....

....

....

[3]

[Total 5 marks]

Exam Practice Tip

One of the most important things to learn about Group 7 elements is the trend you find in reactivity as you go down or up the group. And you need to be able to explain this trend using the electronic structure of the halogens. Smashing.

Topic 6 — Groups in the Periodic Table

Halogen Displacement Reactions

1   Josie investigated the reactions that occur when chlorine, bromine or iodine are added to different sodium halide solutions. **Figure 1** shows her results.

	Sodium chloride solution (NaCl$_{(aq)}$, colourless)	Sodium bromide solution (NaBr$_{(aq)}$, colourless)	Sodium iodide solution (NaI$_{(aq)}$, colourless)
Add chlorine water (Cl$_{2\,(aq)}$, colourless)	no reaction	solution turns orange	....
Add bromine water (Br$_{2\,(aq)}$, orange)	no reaction	....	solution turns brown
Add iodine water (I$_{2\,(aq)}$, brown)	no reaction	no reaction	no reaction

Figure 1

a) Use your knowledge of the reactivity trend of the halogens to fill in the missing results in **Figure 1**.

[2]

b) Explain why there was no reaction when Josie added iodine water to sodium bromide solution.

....

....

[2]

c) i) Construct a balanced symbol equation for the reaction that happened when Josie added chlorine water to sodium bromide solution.

....

[2]

ii) Explain, in terms of electrons, why the reaction between chlorine water and sodium bromide solution can be described as a redox reaction.

....

....

....

[2]

d) Astatine is below iodine in Group 7. Predict whether chlorine water would react with sodium astatide solution. Explain your answer.

....

....

[2]

[Total 10 marks]

Topic 6 — Groups in the Periodic Table

Group 0 — Noble Gases

1 Old-style filament light bulbs contain a thin metal filament. If these light bulbs were filled with air, oxygen would react with the filament causing it to burn away. To avoid this, the light bulbs are filled with argon.

Explain why argon is suitable for this use, including ideas about electronic structure.

....

....

....

....

[Total 3 marks]

2 The noble gases are inert gases that make up Group 0 of the periodic table.

Figure 1 shows some information about the first four noble gases.

Element	Symbol	Boiling point (°C)	Density (kg m^{-3})
Helium	He	−269	0.18
Neon	Ne	−246	0.90
Argon	Ar	−186	?
Krypton	Kr	−153	3.7

Figure 1

a) i) The element below krypton in Group 0 is xenon.
Use the information in **Figure 1** to predict what the boiling point of xenon will be.

boiling point = ... °C
[1]

ii) Use the information in **Figure 1** to predict the density of argon.

density = ... kg m^{-3}
[1]

b) Would you expect the boiling point of radon to be higher or lower than the boiling point of xenon? Explain your answer.

....

....

[1]

[Total 3 marks]

Exam Practice Tip

Make sure you get lots of practice at questions like Q2, where you're given information about some of the elements in a group and asked to use it to predict something about another element in the group. They need careful thinking through.

Topic 6 — Groups in the Periodic Table

Reaction Rate Experiments

1   A scientist reacts hydrochloric acid with marble chips to form calcium chloride, water and carbon dioxide gas.   PRACTICAL

a) He decides to measure the volume of carbon dioxide formed to work out the rate of the reaction. Outline a method the scientist could follow to monitor the volume of gas produced over the course of the reaction.

....

....

....

....

[3]

b) **Figure 1** shows a graph of his results. On **Figure 1**, sketch a curve that shows how the volume of gas produced would change over time if the experiment was carried out at a higher temperature.

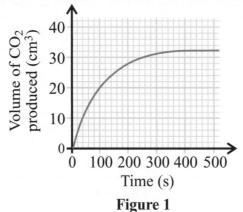

Figure 1

[2]

c) The scientist repeated the reaction using different quantities of reactants. Reaction **X** used 0.500 g of marble chips and an excess of 0.100 mol dm^{-3} hydrochloric acid. Using **Figure 2**, determine which of the following sets of conditions could have resulted in reaction **Y**. Tick **one** box.

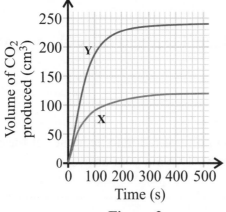

Figure 2

☐ **A** 0.250 g of marble chips and an excess of 0.100 mol dm^{-3} hydrochloric acid.

☐ **B** 1.00 g of marble chips and an excess of 0.100 mol dm^{-3} hydrochloric acid.

☐ **C** 0.250 g of marble chips and an excess of 0.200 mol dm^{-3} hydrochloric acid.

☐ **D** 1.00 g of marble chips and an excess of 0.200 mol dm^{-3} hydrochloric acid.

[1]

[Total 6 marks]

2 Laiza is investigating the effect of temperature on the rate of the reaction between sodium thiosulfate and hydrochloric acid. The reaction forms a cloudy, yellow precipitate of sulfur.

a) She measures out volumes of both reactants and gently heats each of the solutions in a water bath to 50 °C. Outline a method that Laiza could follow to monitor the rate of this reaction.

....

....

....

[3]

b) Laiza repeats the experiment but instead heats both reactant solutions to 30 °C.

i) How would you expect the rate of this reaction to compare to the rate of the reaction at 50 °C?

....

[1]

ii) Name **one** factor Laiza would have to keep the same for both reactions to make it a fair test.

....

[1]

[Total 5 marks]

3 Shabnam reacted magnesium ribbons with hydrochloric acid. As the reaction proceeded, hydrogen gas was produced.

Shabnam carried out two different reactions, **M** and **N**, using two different concentrations of acid in order to see how concentration affects the rate of reaction. All of the other variables were kept the same during both of the experiments. A graph of her results is shown in **Figure 3**.

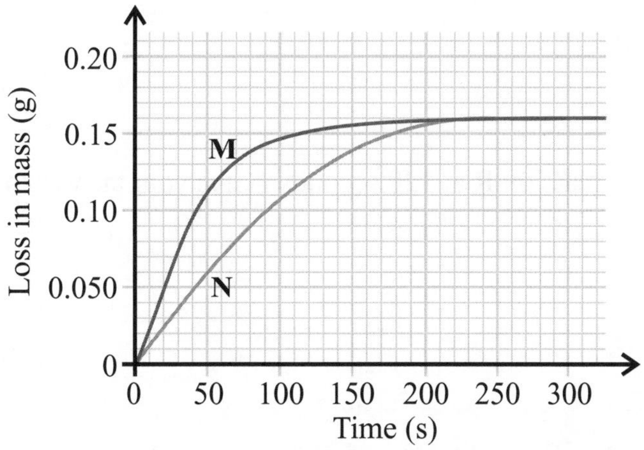

Figure 3

a) Which reaction, **M** or **N**, used a higher concentration of hydrochloric acid? Explain your answer.

....

....

[2]

b) Using the graph, calculate the rate of reaction **N** between 0 and 50 seconds.

rate = ... g s^{-1}

[2]

[Total 4 marks]

Topic 7 — Rates of Reaction and Energy Changes

4   A student wanted to calculate the rate of reaction between nitric acid and zinc. He carried out two experiments under the same conditions, but in one he used zinc ribbons and in the other he used zinc powder.

The graph in **Figure 4** shows the rate of reaction for both experiments, labelled **Q** and **R**.

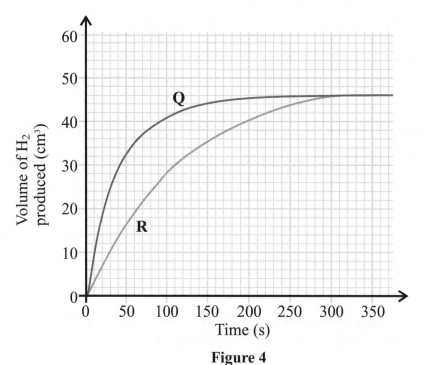

Figure 4

a) i) Calculate the rate of reaction **Q** at 50 seconds. Give your answer to 2 significant figures.

rate = ... cm³ s⁻¹
[3]

ii) Calculate the rate of reaction **R** at 120 seconds. Give your answer to 2 significant figures.

rate = ... cm³ s⁻¹
[3]

b) State which reaction, **Q** or **R**, used the powdered zinc. Explain your answer.

....

....

....
[3]
[Total 9 marks]

Exam Practice Tip

Drawing a tangent at a specific point on a curve can be quite tricky. You need to make sure that it has the same gradient as the curve at that specific point. Drawing a tangent too different from the correct gradient could make a big difference to your final answer, so take your time and try moving your ruler around a bit first to find the best position.

Topic 7 — Rates of Reaction and Energy Changes

Collision Theory

A student is investigating the reaction between nitric acid and calcium carbonate under three different conditions, **A**, **B** and **C**. All other variables are kept the same. Circle the condition that will result in the greatest rate of reaction.

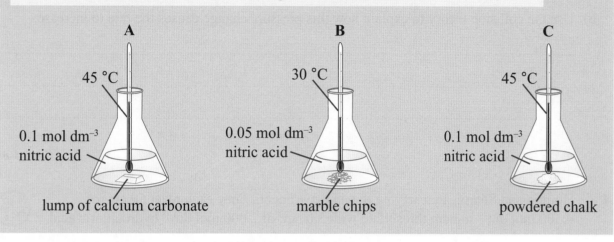

1   This question is about the rate of a chemical reaction between two reactants, one of which is in solution, and one of which is a solid.   Grade 4-6

a) Which of the following changes would **not** cause the rate of the chemical reaction to increase? Tick **one** box.

☐ **A** Increasing the concentration of the solution.

☐ **B** Heating the reaction mixture to a higher temperature.

☐ **C** Using a larger volume of the solution, but keeping the concentration the same.

☐ **D** Grinding the solid reactant so that it forms a fine powder.

[1]

b) What is the name given to the minimum amount of energy which particles must have if they are to react when they collide?

....

[1]

[Total 2 marks]

2   This question is about the rate of the reaction between magnesium and hydrochloric acid. The chemical equation for the reaction is: Grade 6-7

$$Mg_{(s)} + 2HCl_{(aq)} \rightarrow MgCl_{2(aq)} + H_{2(g)}$$

Using collision theory, explain why cutting the magnesium into smaller pieces affects the rate of this reaction.

....

....

....

[Total 2 marks]

3 The Sabatier reaction can be used industrially to make methane from carbon dioxide and hydrogen in the following reaction:

$$CO_{2(g)} + 4H_{2(g)} \rightarrow CH_{4(g)} + 2H_2O_{(g)}$$

a) How could the pressure be altered to **increase** the rate of the reaction?

....
[1]

b) Use the collision theory to explain how this pressure change causes the rate to increase.

....

....

....
[2]

[Total 3 marks]

4 Horatio and Sharon are carrying out an experiment. They each react 50 cm³ of 0.300 mol dm⁻³ sodium thiosulfate with 5.0 cm³ of 2.000 mol dm⁻³ hydrochloric acid.

a) Horatio carries out his reaction at room temperature. Sharon heats her reactants to 45 °C and carries out the reaction in a 45 °C water bath. Horatio thinks that his reaction will have taken place much more quickly than Sharon's reaction. Is Horatio correct? Explain your answer using collision theory.

....

....

....

....

....
[3]

b) i) Sharon repeats her experiment using different concentrations of hydrochloric acid. Which of the following concentrations of hydrochloric acid would result in the **slowest** rate of reaction? Tick **one** box.

☐ **A** 0.350 mol dm⁻³ hydrochloric acid

☐ **B** 1.250 mol dm⁻³ hydrochloric acid

☐ **C** 2.100 mol dm⁻³ hydrochloric acid

☐ **D** 0.550 mol dm⁻³ hydrochloric acid
[1]

ii) Explain your answer.

....

....
[2]

[Total 6 marks]

Topic 7 — Rates of Reaction and Energy Changes

Catalysts

1 Enzymes are a type of catalyst. **Grade 4-6**

   a) Identify which of the following catalysts is an example of an enzyme. Tick **one** box.

     ☐ **A** Iron: a catalyst used in the Haber process.

     ☐ **B** Manganese(IV) oxide: a catalyst used in the decomposition of hydrogen peroxide.

     ☐ **C** RuBisCO: a catalyst used in photosynthesis.

     ☐ **D** Vanadium pentoxide: a catalyst used in the Contact process.

[1]

   b) Give **one** example of when enzymes are used as catalysts in industrial processes.

     ....

[1]

[Total 2 marks]

2 Zola is observing the decomposition of hydrogen peroxide. The reaction is very slow. Meredith tells her to repeat the experiment with manganese(IV) oxide powder, and the rate of reaction increases. **Grade 6-7**

   a) Zola determines that the manganese(IV) oxide must have acted as a catalyst. Explain how a catalyst works to increase the rate of reaction.

     ....

     ....

     ....

[2]

   b) Why does Zola only need to use a small mass of manganese(IV) oxide powder to catalyse the reaction?

     ....

[1]

   c) The reaction profiles for both the catalysed and the uncatalysed reactions are shown in **Figure 1**. Identify what each of the labels, A–D, show.

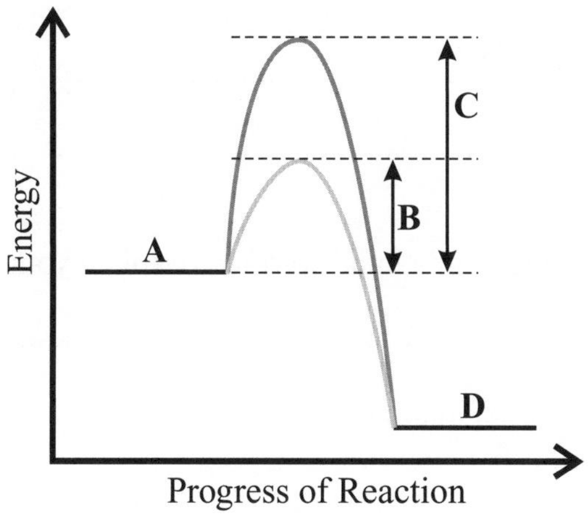

A: ....

B: ....

....

C: ....

....

D: ....

Figure 1

[4]

[Total 7 marks]

Topic 7 — Rates of Reaction and Energy Changes

Endothermic and Exothermic Reactions

1 Which of the following energy changes describes an exothermic reaction? Tick **one** box.

	Energy of products	Temperature of surroundings
A	Greater than reactants	Increases
B	Less than reactants	Increases
C	Greater than reactants	Decreases
D	Less than reactants	Decreases

[Total 1 mark]

2 The thermal decomposition of calcium carbonate is an endothermic reaction.

Sketch and label a reaction profile for this reaction on the axes below. Label the activation energy.

[Total 3 marks]

3 A company is looking for a reaction with a low activation energy to use in a hand warmer.
The reaction profiles for the reactions being investigated are shown in **Figure 1**.

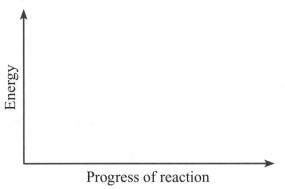

Figure 1

a) Define 'activation energy'.

....

....

[1]

b) Suggest which reaction would be **most suitable** for using in a hand warmer. Explain your answer.

....

....

....

[3]

[Total 4 marks]

Measuring Temperature Changes

1   A student is investigating the temperature change that occurs when he dissolves the same number of moles of two different salts, **A** and **B**, in water.

Grade 6-7

a)   Suggest **three** essential pieces of apparatus needed for the investigation.

....

....

[3]

b)* Describe a method that the student could use to carry out his investigation. Include details of any variables that would need to be controlled.

....

....

....

....

....

....

....

....

....

[6]

c)   The student's results are shown in **Figure 1**. Complete the table.

Salt	Initial temperature (°C)	End temperature (°C)	Temperature change (°C)
A	21.0	16.0	....
B	21.0	26.5	....

Figure 1

[2]

d)   Which of the statements below about the student's experiment is correct? Tick **one** box.

☐   **A**   Both salts dissolved exothermically.

☐   **B**   Salt A dissolved exothermically, but salt B dissolved endothermically.

☐   **C**   Salt A dissolved endothermically, but salt B dissolved exothermically.

☐   **D**   Both salts dissolved endothermically.

[1]

[Total 12 marks]

Bond Energies

Which of the following statements is true? Tick **one** box.

☐ A During exothermic reactions, the energy taken to break the bonds in the reactants is greater than the energy released by making the bonds in the products.

☐ B During endothermic reactions, the energy released by breaking bonds in the reactants is less than the energy taken to make the bonds in the products.

☐ C During exothermic reactions, the energy taken to break the bonds in the reactants is less than the energy released by making the bonds in the products.

☐ D During endothermic reactions, the energy taken to break the bonds in the reactants is less than the energy released by making the bonds in the products.

1   Look at **Figure 1**. It shows the bond energies of some bonds.

Bond	Bond energy (kJ mol⁻¹)
C — H	413
C — O	358
H — O	463
C = C	614
C — C	347

Figure 1

a) Use **Figure 1** to work out the energy change of the following reaction between ethene and water.

$$
\underset{H}{\overset{H}{}}\!\!\!C=C\!\!\!\underset{H}{\overset{H}{}} \;+\; \underset{H}{\overset{}{H}}\!\!-O-H \;\rightarrow\; H-\underset{|\;H}{\overset{H\;|}{C}}-\underset{|\;H}{\overset{H\;|}{C}}-O-H
$$

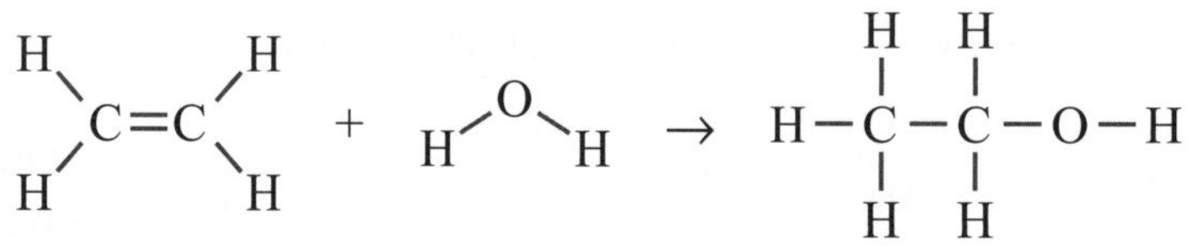

Energy change = ... kJ mol⁻¹

[3]

b) Using your answer to a), state whether the reaction between ethene and water is endothermic or exothermic. Explain your answer.

....

....

[2]

[Total 5 marks]

2 The energy change of the following reaction is –119 kJ mol⁻¹.

H−C−C−H + Cl−Cl → H−C−C−H + H−Cl

a) Compare the energy released by forming bonds in the products
in this reaction with the energy used to break bonds in the reactants.

....

....
[1]

b) Use this information, as well as the data in **Figure 2**,
to work out the approximate bond energy of an H—Cl bond.

Figure 2

Bond	Bond energy (kJ mol⁻¹)
C — H	413
C — C	347
C — Cl	339
Cl — Cl	239

Bond energy = ... kJ mol⁻¹
[3]

c) Use your answer from b) to rank the bonds from **Figure 2**,
and the H—Cl bond in order of strength, from weakest to strongest.

....
[1]

[Total 5 marks]

Exam Practice Tip

In questions involving calculating energy changes from bond energies (or vice versa), it can be really useful to draw out the displayed formulas of the chemicals that you're dealing with (unless you're given them in the question of course). Displayed formulas show all of the atoms in a molecule and all the bonds between them, so doing this makes it much easier to see what bonds have broken and what new bonds have been made during a chemical reaction.

Topic 7 — Rates of Reaction and Energy Changes

Fractional Distillation and Hydrocarbons

Warm-Up

Draw a line to match each of the following fractions of crude oil with one of its main uses.

Bitumen		Fuel for aircraft
Diesel		Surfacing roads and roofs
Kerosene		Fuel for cars and trains.

1   Crude oil is a complex mixture of hydrocarbons.   **Grade 4-6**

a) What is a hydrocarbon?

    ....
    [2]

b) To which homologous series do most of the hydrocarbons in crude oil belong? Tick **one** box.

    ☐ **A** alkenes

    ☐ **B** alkanes

    ☐ **C** alcohols

    ☐ **D** carboxylic acids

    [1]

c) Crude oil is a finite resource. What does this mean?

    ....
    [1]

    [Total 4 marks]

2   The hydrocarbons in crude oil belong to several different homologous series.
     Compounds in a homologous series all share the same general formula.
     Give **three** other characteristics of the compounds in a homologous series.   **Grade 6-7**

....

....

....

....

....

[Total 3 marks]

3 Propane, C_3H_8, is a hydrocarbon present in the gas fraction of crude oil. (Grade 6-7)

a) Propane can be used as a fuel by burning it in oxygen.

   i) Why do hydrocarbons make good fuels?

   ....

   [1]

   ii) Write a balanced symbol equation for the complete combustion of propane.

   ....

   [2]

b) Propane is a very small hydrocarbon molecule. Which of the following statements about propane is **true**? Tick **one** box.

   ☐ **A** It has a low boiling point and is hard to ignite.

   ☐ **B** It has a high boiling point and is easy to ignite.

   ☐ **C** It has a low boiling point and is easy to ignite.

   ☐ **D** It has a high boiling point and is hard to ignite.

[1]

[Total 4 marks]

4 Kerosene, diesel oil and fuel oil are all fractions of crude oil that can be used as fuels. The average chain length of the hydrocarbons in kerosene is shorter than those in diesel oil. The average chain length of the hydrocarbons in diesel oil is shorter than those in fuel oil. (Grade 6-7)

a) State which of the three fractions named above has the highest boiling point. Explain your answer with reference to the information above.

   ....

   ....

   [2]

b) Compare the viscosity of kerosene and fuel oil. Explain your answer with reference to the information above.

   ....

   ....

   [2]

c) Compare the ease of ignition of kerosene and diesel oil. Explain your answer with reference to the information above.

   ....

   ....

   [2]

[Total 6 marks]

Topic 8 — Fuels and Earth Science

5 Crude oil can be separated using the process of fractional distillation. The length of the hydrocarbon chains is fundamental to this process.

Figure 1 shows the boiling points of two molecules that are present in two of the fractions produced by the fractional distillation of crude oil.

Hydrocarbon	Chemical formula	Boiling point (°C)
Heptane	C_7H_{16}	98
Triacontane	$C_{30}H_{62}$	450

Figure 1

a) Triacontane is present in the fuel oil fraction. Give **two** uses of fuel oil.

....

....

[2]

b) i) Which of these two hydrocarbons would you expect to be collected **further down** the fractionating column?

....

[1]

ii) Explain your answer, with reference to the intermolecular forces present between the hydrocarbon molecules.

....

....

....

....

....

....

....

....

[5]

c) A scientist tests the viscosity of heptane, triacontane and a third alkane, alkane **X**. She finds that alkane **X** is more viscous than both heptane and triacontane. Suggest which fraction of crude oil alkane **X** is likely to have been taken from.

....

[1]

[Total 9 marks]

Exam Practice Tip

Remember that if you're given one physical property of a hydrocarbon, you can use it to predict other properties of that compound. For example, if you're told that a certain hydrocarbon has a low boiling point, you can predict that it will have low viscosity, be easy to ignite, and come from a fraction that is collected towards the top of the fractionating column.

Pollutants

1 Acid rain is formed when certain gases dissolve in rainwater to form a dilute acid. **Grade 4-6**

a) Which of the following gases contributes to acid rain? Tick **one** box.

☐ **A** carbon dioxide

☐ **B** methane

☐ **C** sulfur dioxide

☐ **D** carbon monoxide

[1]

b) Give **two** possible negative effects of acid rain.

....

....

[2]

[Total 3 marks]

2 Combustion of fuels, such as petrol, in cars is a major contributor to air pollution. **Grade 6-7**

a) Explain how cars produce nitrogen oxides.

....

....

[2]

b) Fuel combustion can produce soot. What impact can soot have on human health?

....

[1]

c) State which toxic gas is produced by incomplete fuel combustion and explain why it is toxic.

....

....

....

[3]

d) Hydrogen gas can also be used as a fuel in cars. Give **two** advantages of
using hydrogen gas rather than fossil fuels as a means of powering vehicles.

....

....

....

[2]

[Total 8 marks]

 ☐   ☐   ☐

Topic 8 — Fuels and Earth Science

Cracking

1 Some hydrocarbons from crude oil undergo processing by the petrochemical industry. For instance, decane, $C_{10}H_{22}$, can undergo cracking as shown in the following equation:

$$C_{10}H_{22} \rightarrow C_8H_{18} + C_2H_4$$

Grade 6-7

a) C_2H_4 is an unsaturated hydrocarbon. To which homologous series does it belong? Tick **one** box.

☐ **A** alkanes ☐ **B** alkenes ☐ **C** alcohols ☐ **D** carboxylic acids

[1]

b) Explain why a petrochemical company may need to crack hydrocarbons.

....

....

[2]

c) Cracking can form a variety of products.
Write an alternative balanced equation for the cracking of decane.

....

[1]

[Total 4 marks]

2 The hydrocarbon fractions produced by the fractional distillation of crude oil are used in many industrial processes. **Figure 1** shows the approximate percentage of each fraction produced by an oil refinery and the demand for each fraction.

Grade 6-7

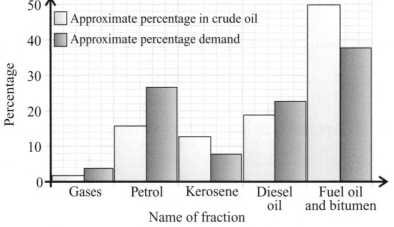

Figure 1

a) The demand for diesel oil is greater than the supply. Using **Figure 1**, name **two** other fractions whose demand is greater than their supply.

....

[2]

b) Suggest what could be done to help match the supply of diesel oil to the demand.

....

....

[1]

[Total 3 marks]

Topic 8 — Fuels and Earth Science

The Atmosphere

1   Which of these statements about Earths's early atmosphere is **correct**? Tick **one** box. Grade 4-6

   ☐ **A** The gases that made up Earth's early atmosphere were released by volcanic eruptions.

   ☐ **B** The Earth's oceans were formed when the methane in the early atmosphere condensed.

   ☐ **C** Earth's early atmosphere contained less carbon dioxide than the atmosphere today.

   ☐ **D** Earth's early atmosphere contained a lot of oxygen.

[Total 1 mark]

2   Scientists have looked at the compositions of the atmospheres of other planets to provide evidence for what the early atmosphere on Earth was like. Grade 6-7
Figure 1 shows the current compositions of the atmospheres on Mars and Earth.

	Percentage composition (%)					
	H_2O	Ne	CO_2	N_2	O_2	Ar
Mars	0.030	trace	95	2.7	0.13	1.6
Earth	0–4.0	0.0018	0.036	78	21	0.93

Figure 1

a) i) Scientists believe Earth's early atmosphere was similar to the atmosphere on Mars.
      Using **Figure 1**, suggest which gas made up the majority of Earth's early atmosphere.

   ....
[1]

   ii) Explain **two** ways in which this gas was removed from Earth's atmosphere as it evolved.

   ....

   ....
[2]

b) i) Explain how oxygen built up in Earth's atmosphere and suggest
      why there is hardly any oxygen present in the atmosphere of Mars.

   ....

   ....

   ....
[2]

   ii) Describe the chemical test for oxygen.

   ....
[1]

[Total 6 marks]

Topic 8 — Fuels and Earth Science

The Greenhouse Effect and Climate Change

Identify the statements below that describe things that a family can do to reduce their carbon dioxide emissions. Tick **two** boxes.

Leaving lights on all day	☐	Using a tumble drier	☐
Walking to school	☐	Turning central heating down	☐
Leaving appliances on standby	☐	Using air conditioning	☐

1 The Earth's atmosphere contains greenhouse gases which contribute to the greenhouse effect. *(Grade 4-6)*

a) Name **two** greenhouse gases.

....
[2]

b) Give **two** examples of types of human activity which are leading to an **increase** in the concentration of greenhouse gases in the atmosphere.

....

....
[2]

[Total 4 marks]

2 The Earth absorbs some electromagnetic radiation from the sun. It then radiates some of the radiation it absorbs as infrared (IR) radiation. IR radiation contributes to the greenhouse effect by interacting with greenhouse gases. *(Grade 6-7)*

a) Which of the following statements is **true**? Tick **one** box.

☐ **A** Greenhouse gases absorb all of the IR radiation that is radiated by Earth.

☐ **B** The greenhouse effect is caused by the absorption and reflection of IR radiation by greenhouse gases.

☐ **C** In general, the higher the concentration of greenhouse gases in the Earth's atmosphere, the colder the Earth becomes.

☐ **D** Greenhouse gases make up a large percentage of Earth's current atmosphere.

[1]

b) Elvis says he thinks that any amount of any greenhouse gases in the Earth's atmosphere is dangerous, as it could cause global warming. Is Elvis correct? Explain your answer.

....

....
[1]

[Total 2 marks]

3 Some scientists believe that the increased burning of fossil fuels has contributed to global warming and this has caused glaciers to melt, resulting in rising sea levels. Other scientists believe that the rises in global temperature are just natural fluctuations.

Figure 1 shows CO_2 emissions by fossil fuels in the UK and Crown dependencies and the changes in sea levels between 1993 and 2013.

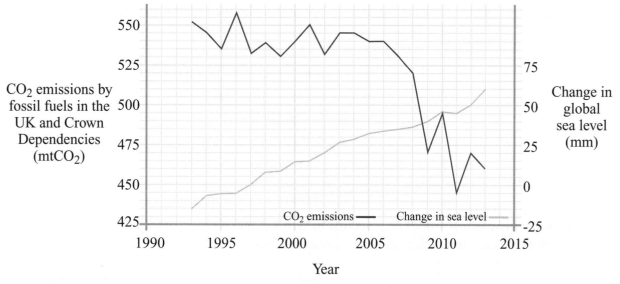

Figure 1

a)* Look at **Figure 1**. Explain whether the data shown on this graph supports a link between human activity and climate change. Discuss any problems associated with using this data to draw conclusions about the affect of carbon dioxide emissions on global sea levels.

....

....

....

....

....

....

....

....

[6]

b) Many governments are trying to decrease their country's CO_2 emissions.
   Give **two** ways that the government in the UK is trying to reduce carbon dioxide emissions.

....

....

[2]

[Total 8 marks]

Exam Practice Tip

You could be given data that shows a link between human activity and global warming. But, just because there might be a correlation, it doesn't necessarily mean that one causes the other. You need to evaluate what the data actually shows without making assumptions. For example, if you're given data for one country, you can't assume it's had a global effect.

Topic 8 — Fuels and Earth Science

Tests for Ions

1   Kelly has a small bottle of a clear solution labelled 'ammonium sulfate solution'. Her teacher asks her to perform some tests to confirm that the bottle of solution has been correctly labelled.

a)   First, Kelly tests the solution for ammonium ions using the method shown in **Figure 1**.

> Method for testing for ammonium ions
> 1. Place 3 cm³ of your test solution in a test tube.
> 2. Add 3 cm³ of sodium hydroxide solution.
> 3. Warm the mixture gently.
> 4. Collect any gas that is given off.
> 5. Test the gas you have collected.

Figure 1

i)   Name the gas that would be given off in step 4 if the solution being tested did contain ammonium ions.

....

[1]

ii)   Describe how Kelly should test for this gas in step 5, and describe what a positive result would look like.

....

....

....

[2]

b)   Next, Kelly tests the solution for sulfate ions using the method shown in **Figure 2**.

> Method for testing for sulfate ions
> 1. Place 3 cm³ of your test solution in a test tube.
> 2. Add 3 cm³ of hydrochloric acid.
> 3. Add 10 drops of Reagent **X** to the test tube and observe what happens.

Figure 2

Kelly's test solution does contain sulfate ions.
When she adds Reagent **X** to the test solution in step 3, a precipitate forms.

i)   Identify Reagent **X**.

....

[1]

ii)   State the colour of the precipitate that forms when Reagent **X** is added in step 3.

....

[1]

[Total 5 marks]

2 Various tests can be used to identify which metal ion is present in a compound. *(Grade 4-6)*

a) Suggest what metal ion is present in a compound that, when heated in a flame, produces a red flame.

....

[1]

b) Copper(II) nitrate is a soluble salt that contains copper(II) ions.

i) What colour flame would you expect this compound to produce during a flame test?

....

[1]

ii) If you dissolved copper(II) nitrate in water and then added a few drops of sodium hydroxide, what would you expect to observe?

....

[2]

[Total 4 marks]

3 Mark is given samples of three solutions, **A**, **B**, and **C**. Each solution contains a metal compound. He tests separate samples of each of the solutions with acidified silver nitrate solution and sodium hydroxide solution. His results are shown in **Figure 3**. *(Grade 6-7)*

Test	Observation		
	Solution A	**Solution B**	**Solution C**
Add acidified silver nitrate solution	yellow precipitate forms	no reaction	cream precipitate forms
Add a few drops of sodium hydroxide solution	white precipitate forms	brown precipitate forms	green precipitate forms

Figure 3

a) Suggest which metal ion solution **B** contains.

....

[1]

b) Suggest the formula of the compound in solution **C**.

....

[1]

c) i) After adding sodium hydroxide to solution **A**, Mark says "I can tell from my results that solution **A** contains aluminium ions." Explain why Mark is **wrong**.

....

....

[1]

ii) If solution **A** did contain aluminium ions, what would you expect Mark to observe if he added more sodium hydroxide solution to the test tube?

....

[1]

[Total 4 marks]

4 The compound potassium sodium carbonate has the formula $KNaCO_3$. `Grade 6-7`

a) Explain why it would be difficult to identify the cations in this compound using a flame test.

....

....

[1]

b) Describe how you could test a solution of this compound to show that it contained carbonate ions. You should include details of a positive result.

....

....

....

....

[3]

[Total 4 marks]

5* Oliver was asked to prepare a sample of potassium chloride. He designed a suitable method and carried it out. When he had finished, he had 5 g of the solid salt. `Grade 7-9`

Describe how Oliver could show that the salt he has made is potassium chloride. In your answer you should give the methods for any tests that you suggest and details of any observations you would expect to confirm the presence of the ions in the salt.

....

....

....

....

....

....

....

....

....

....

....

[Total 6 marks]

Exam Practice Tip

The examiner might ask you to identify a salt in solution by looking at the results of different tests. Remember, a salt will contain both an anion and a cation, so if your answer only has ions with the <u>same</u> charge, you've probably made a mistake.

Topic 9 — Separate Chemistry 2

Flame Photometry

1 Flame photometry is an example of an instrumental method of analysis. Which of the following statements about instrumental methods is **false**? Tick **one** box.

Grade 4-6

☐ **A** Instrumental methods are very slow.

☐ **B** Instrumental methods are sensitive, so only a small amount of a sample is needed.

☐ **C** Instrumental methods can be more accurate than using standard laboratory tests.

☐ **D** Instrumental methods are reliant on machinery.

[Total 1 mark]

2 A chemist has a dilute solution, **M**, containing metal ions. She tests the solution using flame photometry. **Figure 1** shows the line spectra for metal **A**, metal **B**, metal **C** and the solution, **M**.

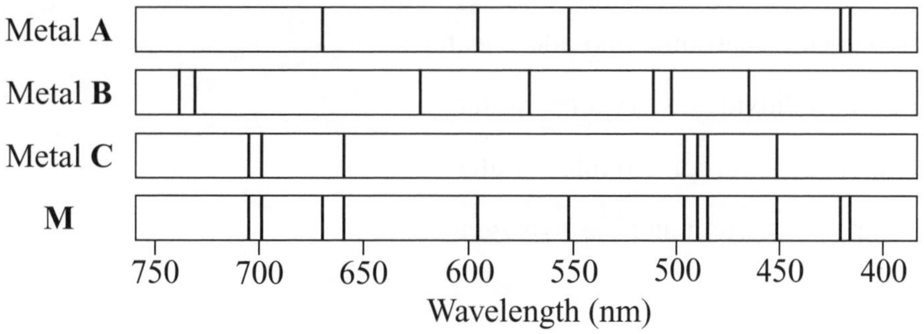

Grade 6-7

Metal **A**

Metal **B**

Metal **C**

M

750   700   650   600   550   500   450   400
Wavelength (nm)

Figure 1

a) Which metal ion(s) are in the solution, **M**?

....

[1]

b) The chemist produces a calibration curve for an ion present in solution **M**. The ion emits a certain wavelength of light with a relative emission intensity of 3.6. Use the calibration curve in **Figure 2** to work out the concentration of the ion in solution **M**.

Figure 2

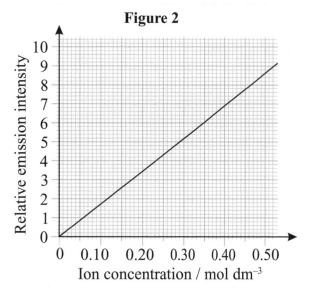

Relative emission intensity

10
9
8
7
6
5
4
3
2
1
0

0   0.10   0.20   0.30   0.40   0.50
Ion concentration / mol dm⁻³

Concentration = ... mol dm⁻³

[1]

[Total 2 marks]

Topic 9 — Separate Chemistry 2

Alkanes and Alkenes

Warm-Up

Circle the organic compounds below which are **unsaturated**.

H–C–H (with H above and below central C)   H₂C=CH₂ type structure   H–C–C–C–H (with H's)   H–C–C–C–O–H (with H's)   C=C branched structure with CH₃ groups

1   Alkanes and alkenes can take part in complete combustion reactions.

Which of the following shows the **correct** word equation
for the complete combustion of ethene? Tick **one** box.

☐ **A** ethene + oxygen → carbon monoxide + water

☐ **B** ethene + carbon dioxide → oxygen + water

☐ **C** ethene + oxygen → carbon dioxide + water

☐ **D** ethene + water → carbon dioxide + oxygen

[Total 1 mark]

2   Alkanes are a homologous series of hydrocarbons.

a) i) Name the alkane that contains **two** carbon atoms.

    ....

[1]

ii) State the number of hydrogen atoms that this alkane contains.

    ....

[1]

b) Draw the displayed formula of butane.

[1]

c) Alkanes can be described as '**saturated**'. What does the term **saturated** mean?

    ....

    ....

[1]

[Total 4 marks]

3 A student is investigating the chemical structure of alkenes. **Grade 6-7**

a) Give the general formula for alkenes.

....

[1]

b) Identify the displayed formula below that shows ethene. Tick **one** box.

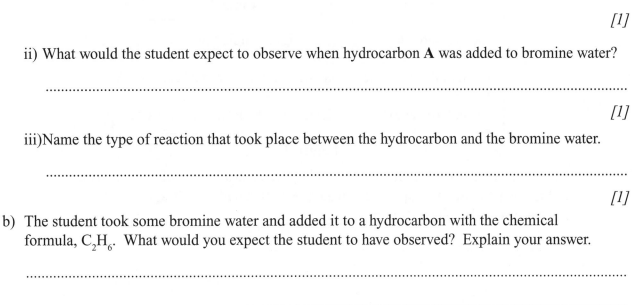

[1]

c) Methane is an alkane with one carbon atom. The student notices that there is not an alkene with only one carbon atom. Explain why an alkene with one carbon atom does **not** exist.

....

....

[1]

[Total 3 marks]

4 A student investigated the reactivity of some hydrocarbons. **Grade 7-9**

a) The student added a sample of a hydrocarbon, **A**, to bromine water. A reaction took place.

i) The chemical formula of the product formed was $C_3H_6Br_2$.
   Draw the displayed formula of hydrocarbon **A**.

[1]

ii) What would the student expect to observe when hydrocarbon **A** was added to bromine water?

....

[1]

iii) Name the type of reaction that took place between the hydrocarbon and the bromine water.

....

[1]

b) The student took some bromine water and added it to a hydrocarbon with the chemical formula, C_2H_6. What would you expect the student to have observed? Explain your answer.

....

....

[3]

[Total 6 marks]

Topic 9 — Separate Chemistry 2

Addition Polymers

1 The following question is about addition polymers. (Grade 6-7)

a) Which of these homologous series can form addition polymers? Tick **one** box.

☐ **A** alkenes and alkanes

☐ **B** alkenes only

☐ **C** carboxylic acids only

☐ **D** alcohols and carboxylic acids

[1]

b) The formula of vinyl acetate is shown in **Figure 1**.
Vinyl acetate polymerises to form poly(vinyl acetate).
Draw the formula of the repeating unit of poly(vinyl acetate).

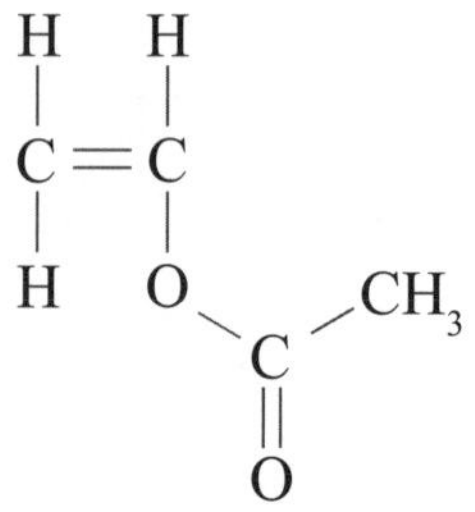

Figure 1

[1]

c) The formula of the repeating unit of poly(propene) is shown
in **Figure 2**. Draw the formula of its monomer.

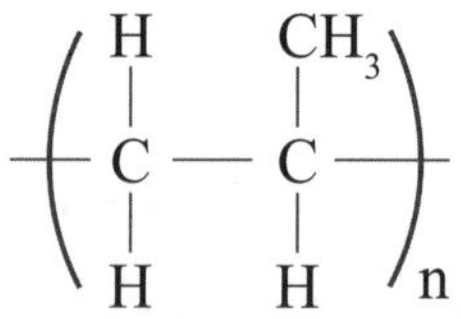

Figure 2

[1]

d) **Figure 3** shows some of the properties of three different addition polymers.

Polymer	Properties
poly(chloroethene)	rigid, tough, low cost
poly(tetrafluoroethene)	non-stick, unreactive, heat-resistance
poly(ethene)	flexible, high electrical resistivity

Figure 3

A designer is trying to decide on a material to use in the production of a frying pan.
Using **Figure 3** choose the material that would be best suited
for this purpose and explain your answer.

....

....

....

[3]

[Total 6 marks]

2 A class are carrying out an investigation to look at monomers and addition polymers.

a) The students are shown the displayed formula of the monomer methyl methacrylate. This monomer is shown in **Figure 4**. Selena believes that it can form an addition polymer but Jenna disagrees. State which student you agree with and why.

H   CH$_3$
| |
C = C
| |
H   C = O
       |
       O — CH$_3$

Figure 4

....

....

[1]

b) The students study poly(tetrafluoroethene), PTFE.
The repeating unit of this polymer is shown in **Figure 5**.

$$\left(\begin{array}{cc} F & F \\ | & | \\ C & - C \\ | & | \\ F & F \end{array}\right)_n$$

Figure 5

Which of the monomers below forms the polymer, poly(tetrafluoroethene)? Tick **one** box.

□ **A**
F   F
| |
H — C — C — H
| |
F   F

□ **B**
F   F
  \   /
   C = C
  /   \
F   F

□ **C**
F   F
  \   /
   C = C
  /   \
H   H

□ **D**
F   F
| |
H — C — C — H
| |
H   H

[1]

c) The addition polymer poly(chloroethene), PVC, can be represented by the notation $(C_2H_3Cl)_n$.
Draw the displayed formula for the monomer that polymerises to form PVC.

[1]

[Total 3 marks]

Exam Practice Tip

The monomers of addition polymers must have a C=C bond, but when they form polymers, this double bond becomes a single bond. Carbon always has four bonds, so if you're drawing the repeating unit of a polymer, count how many bonds your carbon atoms have. This way, you can check the bonds to make sure they're all present and correct.

Topic 9 — Separate Chemistry 2

Condensation Polymers

1 Which of the following molecules **cannot** take part in condensation polymerisation reactions? Tick **one** box.

☐ **A**

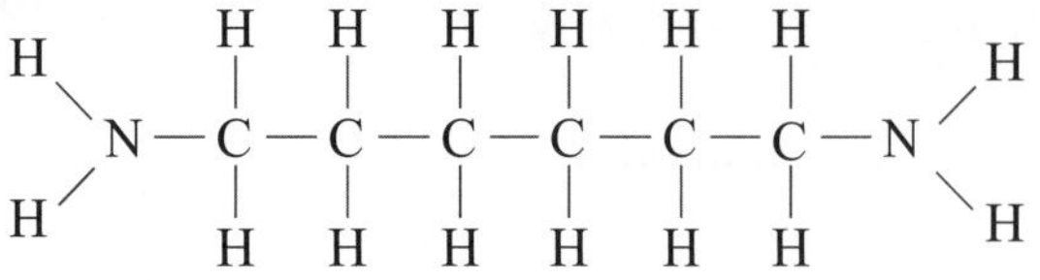

H₂N—CH₂—CH₂—CH₂—CH₂—CH₂—CH₂—NH₂

☐ **B**

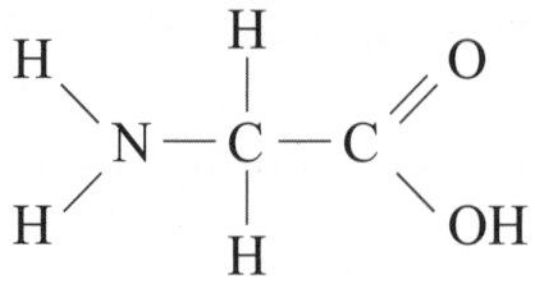

H₂N—CH₂—COOH

☐ **C**

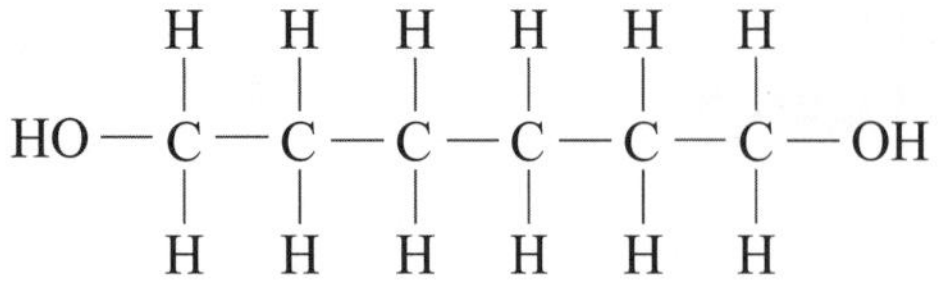

HO—CH₂—CH₂—CH₂—CH₂—CH₂—CH₂—OH

☐ **D**

H—CH₂—CH=CH—CH₂—H

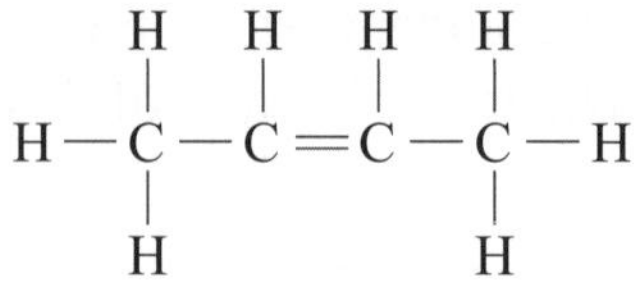

[Total 1 mark]

2 Which of the following is **true** regarding the formation of condensation polymers? Tick **one** box.

☐ **A** A small molecule is lost when condensation polymers form.

☐ **B** Each monomer contains only one functional group.

☐ **C** The monomers must have a carbon-carbon double bond.

☐ **D** The functional groups contained in each monomer must be different.

[Total 1 mark]

3 Some condensation polymers occur naturally and are essential to our growth and survival.

a) Complete the table in **Figure 1** with the names of the types of monomer that form protein and starch polymers.

Polymer	Protein	Starch
Monomer	....	....

Figure 1

[2]

b) i) Nucleotides are a type of monomer that produce another naturally occurring polymer. Name the polymer that is formed from nucleotides.

....

[1]

ii) State how many different types of nucleotide make up this polymer.

....

[1]

[Total 4 marks]

4 A certain condensation polymerisation reaction involving two
different monomers produces a polyester, **D**, and another product, **E**.

a) Which of the following sets of molecules would react to form a polyester? Tick **one** box.

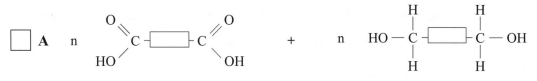

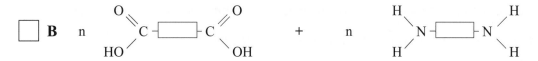

[1]

b) What is the name for the link that is formed between two
monomer molecules during the formation of polyesters?

....

[1]

c) Draw a block diagram showing the repeat unit of a polyester.

[2]

d) i) What is the formula of the product, **E**?

....

[1]

ii) Describe how product **E** is formed.

....

....

[2]

e) Some polyesters are carbohydrates. Name the **three** elements that are present in carbohydrates.

....

[1]

[Total 8 marks]

Topic 9 — Separate Chemistry 2

Disposing of Polymers

1 The following question is about recycling polymers. (Grade 6-7)

a) Which of the following statements about the recycling of polymers is **false**? Tick **one** box.

☐ **A** Increasing the amount of polymers that are recycled can create more jobs.

☐ **B** Recycling polymers means that less polymers need to be disposed of in landfill.

☐ **C** Recycling polymers is generally cheaper than making polymers from scratch.

☐ **D** Polymers can be recycled an infinite number of times.

[1]

b) If we don't recycle polymers, the production of new polymers in the future could be limited. Explain why this is the case.

....

....
[1]

c) Some polymers with particularly high strengths are used in the manufacture of bulletproof vests and prosthetic limbs. Explain why it may be better to manufacture brand new polymers for such uses, rather than using recycled polymers.

....

....
[2]

[Total 4 marks]

2 There are various ways to dispose of polymers. These include recycling, landfill and combustion. (Grade 6-7)

a) When polymers are recycled, they are melted down and reformed. Explain why polymers need to be separated before they're melted down and reformed.

....

....
[1]

b) Give **one** disadvantage of disposing of polymers in landfill.

....

....
[1]

c) Polymers can also be disposed of by combustion. Give **one** advantage and **one** disadvantage of burning polymers.

Advantage: ....

Disadvantage: ....
[2]

[Total 4 marks]

Topic 9 — Separate Chemistry 2

Alcohols and Carboxylic Acids

Warm-Up

Identify which of the following functional groups represents **alcohols**. Tick **one** box.

C = C ☐   -COO⁻ ☐

-NO₂ ☐   -OH ☐

-COOH ☐   -NH₃ ☐

---

1   Three of the following structures belong to the same homologous series.
Identify the structure that belongs to a **different** homologous series. Tick **one** box.

  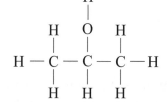

[Total 1 mark]

---

2   Alcohols are a series of organic compounds with a wide range of industrial applications.

a)   An alcohol containing three carbons is commonly used as a solvent.
What is the name given to this alcohol?

....

[1]

b)   Ethanol is present in alcoholic drinks. Give the molecular formula of ethanol.

....

[1]

c)   Methanol can be used as an additive to fuels to improve combustion.
Draw the displayed formula for methanol.

[1]

[Total 3 marks]

3 Under certain conditions, alcohols can be oxidised to form carboxylic acids.

a) What is the functional group of a carboxylic acid?

....
[1]

b) Give the molecular formula of propanoic acid.

....
[1]

c) Name the carboxylic acid with the chemical formula CH_3COOH.

....
[1]

d) Methanol is mixed with an oxidising agent.
Draw the displayed formula of the product that is formed.

[2]
[Total 5 marks]

4 A student mixes butanoic acid with reactant **X** and forms a compound known as an ester.
The student then mixes reactant **X** with other organic compounds.

a) Predict which of the compounds below will also form
an ester when mixed with reactant **X**. Tick **one** box.

☐ **A**
H — C — C — C — C — O — H
(with H atoms above and below each of the four carbons)

☐ **B**
H — C — C — C with =O and O—H
(with H atoms on the first two carbons)

☐ **C**
H — C — C — C — C — C with =O and H
(with H atoms on the four carbons)

☐ **D**
H — C — C — C — C — H with =O on second carbon, O above
(with H atoms on the carbons)

[1]

b) Explain your answer.

....

....

....
[2]
[Total 3 marks]

Topic 9 — Separate Chemistry 2

Production of Ethanol

1 Fermentation is a process that uses yeast to convert glucose to ethanol. (Grade 6-7)

a) Name the other product that is formed in this fermentation reaction.

....
[1]

b) A fermentation reaction produces a dilute solution of ethanol, **X**.
Name the technique that can be used to produce a more concentrated solution
of ethanol from solution **X**, and outline how this process works.

....

....

....

....

....
[5]

[Total 6 marks]

2 Isla and Umar are both carrying out fermentation reactions in the lab. (Grade 6-7)

a) Umar carries her reaction out at 33 °C. Isla thinks that if she carries out her fermentation reaction
at 50 °C, the rate of fermentation will increase. Do you agree with Isla? Explain your answer.

....

....
[2]

b) Umar carries out her reaction in a flask that is open to the air,
whereas Isla carries her experiment out in **anaerobic** conditions.

i) Explain what is meant by **anaerobic** conditions.

....
[1]

ii) Predict the pH of the solution that Umar's fermentation reaction produces. Explain your answer.

....

....
[2]

c) Isla thinks that if she leaves her fermentation mixture for long enough, she can produce
a solution of ethanol with a concentration of 40%. Explain why she is **incorrect**.

....

....

....
[2]

[Total 7 marks]

Topic 9 — Separate Chemistry 2

PRACTICAL

Combustion of Alcohols

1 Manveer is investigating the efficiency of three unknown alcohols, **X**, **Y** and **Z**, as fuels. **Grade 7-9**

a)* Describe a method that Manveer could use to determine which of these alcohols is the most efficient fuel. Include steps that he should take to ensure that a fair test is carried out.

....

....

....

....

....

....

....

....

....

....

....

....

[6]

b) Manveer measures how much of each alcohol is needed to raise the temperature of a set volume of water by 25 °C. His results are shown in **Figure 1**.

Figure 1

Alcohol	X	Y	Z
Mass of fuel burned (g)	1.53	2.19	1.76

i) Using **Figure 1**, determine which of the alcohols, **X**, **Y** or **Z**, was the most efficient fuel. Explain your answer.

....

....

[1]

ii) The longer the carbon chain of an alcohol, the more efficient it will be as a fuel. Manveer was told that the three alcohols were ethanol, propanol and butanol. Assuming that Manveer carried out a fair test, identify which of the alcohols, **X**, **Y** or **Z**, is butanol.

....

[1]

[Total 8 marks]

Nanoparticles

1 Which of the following statements about nanoparticles is **true**? Tick **one** box. (Grade 4-6)

☐ **A** Nanoparticles contain approximately one thousand atoms.

☐ **B** Nanoparticles are 1-100 nm in size.

☐ **C** All nanoparticles are the same size and shape.

☐ **D** Nanoparticles are smaller than simple molecules, such as carbon dioxide.

[Total 1 mark]

2 Nanoparticles of zinc oxide are used in some sunscreens to improve the protection of skin from exposure to sunlight. (Grade 4-6)

State **one** advantage and **one** disadvantage of using nanoparticles of zinc oxide in sunscreens.

Advantage: ....

Disadvantage: ....

[Total 2 marks]

3 Nanomedicine is the name given to the use of nanoparticles to treat illnesses. (Grade 6-7)

a) A scientist says "Nanomedicine could bring great benefits in the future."
Describe **one** example of a possible use of nanoparticles in medicine.
State what property of the nanoparticles you have named makes them suitable for that use.

....

....

....

[2]

b) Another scientist says "We should be cautious about using nanomedicine."
Suggest why this statement might be considered correct.

....

....

....

[2]

[Total 4 marks]

4 Explain how the small size of nanoparticles gives them different properties from larger particles of the same material. (Grade 6-7)

....

....

....

....

[Total 3 marks]

Topic 9 — Separate Chemistry 2

Types of Material and Their Uses

Materials can be categorised into several different types.
Match each of the materials below with the group of materials that it belongs to.

Glass	Metal
Polystyrene	Polymer
Aluminium	Composite
Concrete	Ceramic

1   The uses of materials are determined by their properties.
    Figure 1 shows the properties of some materials.

Material	Stiffness	Electrical Conductivity	Cost
Plasticised PVC	Low	Low	Low
Fibreglass	High	Low	Medium
High-density poly(ethene)	High	Low	Low
Aluminium	High	High	Medium

Figure 1

a) Which material from **Figure 1** is a composite material?

....

[1]

b) Which material from the table in **Figure 1** would be the **most** suitable
    for covering electrical wires to insulate them? Explain your answer.

....

....

....

....

[4]

c) Low-density poly(ethene) is a low cost material with low stiffness and low electrical conductivity.
    Suggest whether high-density poly(ethene) or low-density poly(ethene) would be more suitable for
    making a squeezy ketchup bottle. Explain your answer.

....

....

[1]

[Total 6 marks]

2 **Figure 2** shows the properties of several different materials.

Material	Density (g cm⁻³)	Strength (MPa)	Resistance to Corrosion	Cost
PVC	1.3	52	Good	Low
Carbon fibre	1.5	4100	Good	High
Copper	8.9	220	Poor	Medium
Steel	7.8	780	Poor, but easy to protect	Low
Lead	11.3	12	Good	Low

Figure 2

a) A sports company is choosing a material for a professional hockey stick. Which material from the table would be the **most** suitable? Use data from **Figure 2** to explain your answer.

....

....

....

....

....

[4]

b) Determine which material from the table is the **most** suitable for building bridges. Explain your answer using information from **Figure 2**.

....

....

....

....

....

[4]

c) Determine which material from the table would be the **most** suitable material to make drain pipes. Explain your answer using information from **Figure 2**.

....

....

....

....

....

[4]

[Total 12 marks]

Exam Practice Tip

You may need to decide, out of a choice of materials, which one is the most suitable for making something. Although physical properties are important, don't forget to look at cost. For example, carbon fibre is very strong but also very expensive — if you need to use a lot of it, like for building bridges, it'll cost a lot and this can sometimes be a problem.

Mixed Questions

1 Fractional distillation separates crude oil into fractions. *(Grade 4-6)*

a) In a fractionating column, gaseous molecules turn into liquids
at certain points in the column, where they can be siphoned off.
What is the name given to the change of state when gases turn to liquids?

....

[1]

b) Which of the following fractions is extracted **above** petrol in the fractionating column?
Tick **one** box.

☐ **A** Kerosene   ☐ **B** Gases   ☐ **C** Diesel Oil   ☐ **D** Fuel Oil

[1]

[Total 2 marks]

2 Look at **Figure 1**. It shows the displayed formula of an organic compound. *(Grade 4-6)*

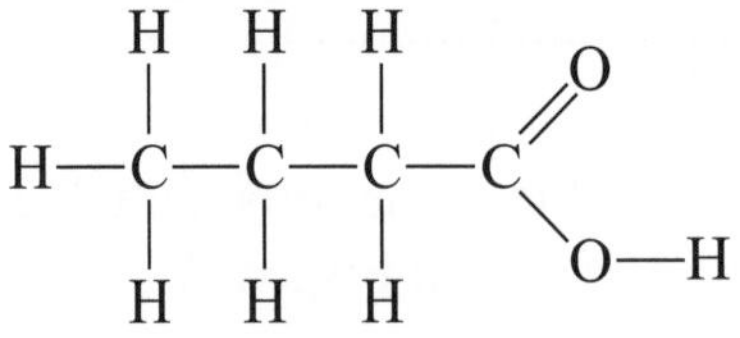

Figure 1

a) Which homologous series does this compound belong to?

....

[1]

b) What is the name of this compound?

....

[1]

c) Find the relative formula mass of this compound.
(relative atomic masses: C = 12, H = 1, O = 16)

relative formula mass = ...

[1]

d) What is the empirical formula of this compound?

....

[2]

[Total 5 marks]

3 Calcium, Ca, and sulfuric acid, H_2SO_4, react together in a chemical reaction. **Grade 4-6**

a) Write a word equation for this reaction.

....
[2]

b) What is the chemical formula of the salt formed by this reaction?

....
[1]

c) Predict whether the salt formed will be soluble or insoluble.

....
[2]

d) The reaction of sulfuric acid with calcium is less violent than its reaction with sodium.
What does this tell you about the position of sodium, relative to calcium, in the reactivity series?

....
[1]

[Total 6 marks]

4 Chlorine is a Group 7 element that exists as molecules of Cl_2. **Grade 4-6**

a) Complete **Figure 2** to give a dot-and-cross diagram that shows the bonding in Cl_2.
You only need to show the outer electron shells.

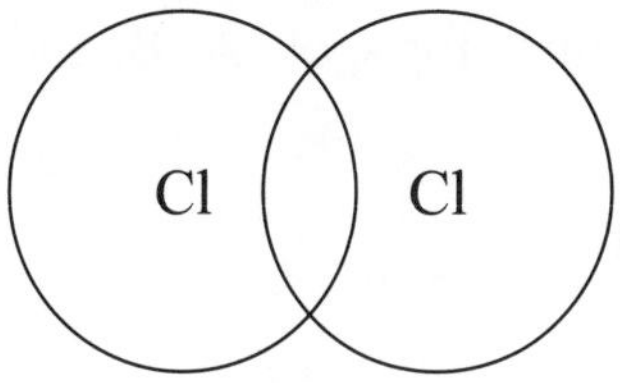

Figure 2 *[2]*

b) Which of the following **best** describes the structure of chlorine?
Tick **one** box.

☐ **A** Giant ionic lattice   ☐ **C** Simple molecular substance

☐ **B** Giant covalent structure   ☐ **D** Fullerene

[1]

c) Describe a test you could carry out for chlorine. Include any observations you would expect.

....

....

....
[2]

d) Chlorine has a melting point of −102 °C and a boiling point of −34 °C.
Predict what state chlorine would be in at −50 °C.

....
[1]

[Total 6 marks]

Mixed Questions

5   Ellie is using paper chromatography experiment to analyse the components in a sample.
     Figure 3 shows the chromatogram produced by the experiment.

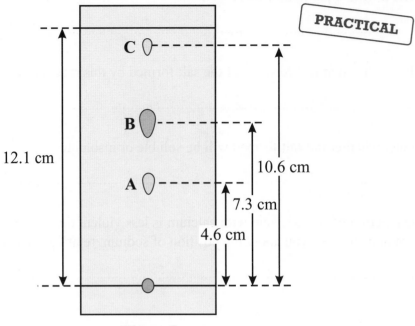

Figure 3

a) Identify the **stationary phase** in Ellie's experiment.

....

[1]

b) Use **Figure 3** to calculate the R_f values for spots **A**, **B**, and **C**.

$$R_f = \frac{\text{distance travelled by solute}}{\text{distance travelled by solvent}}$$

R_f of **A** = ...

R_f of **B** = ...

R_f of **C** = ...

[3]

c) From **Figure 3**, how can you tell that Ellie's sample contains
    a substance that is insoluble in the mobile phase?

....

[1]

d) Use **Figure 3** to identify the **minimum** number of components in Ellie's sample. Tick **one** box.

☐ **A** 1   ☐ **B** 2   ☐ **C** 3   ☐ **D** 4

[1]

e) Ellie concludes that her sample is a mixture. Explain what is meant by the term 'mixture'.

....

....

[1]

f) The mixture contains some liquid components with similar boiling points.
    Name a technique that Ellie could use to separate the different components in the mixture.

....

[1]

[Total 8 marks]

Mixed Questions

6 Zayn carries out an experiment to investigate using alcohols as fuels. During his experiment, he heats a set volume of water by combusting equal masses of some alcohols. He measures the change in temperature of the water.

a) Some of Zayn's results are shown in **Figure 4**.
Complete **Figure 4** to show the temperature change of the water for each reaction.

Alcohol	Starting temperature (°C)	Highest temperature reached (°C)	Temperature change (°C)
Methanol	25.7	42.9	....
Ethanol	25.9	54.3	....
Propanol	26.4	58.9	....

Figure 4

[2]

b) Combustion reactions are exothermic. Use the axes in **Figure 5** to draw a reaction profile for the combustion of an alcohol in oxygen.

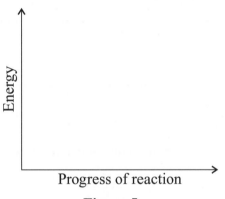

Figure 5

[2]

c) The combustion of alcohols can produce the toxic gas carbon monoxide. Explain why carbon monoxide is toxic.

....

....

[2]

[Total 6 marks]

7 Cracking is an important industrial process. During a certain reaction, one molecule of $C_{25}H_{52}$ was cracked. One of the products was $C_{20}H_{42}$.

a) Write the chemical formula of the other product.

....

[1]

b) The mixture of products produced when $C_{25}H_{52}$ was cracked reaction was shaken with bromine water. Predict what you would observe. Explain your answer.

....

....

[2]

[Total 3 marks]

Mixed Questions

8   **Figure 6** lists some properties of four materials.

Material	Density (g cm⁻³)	Brittleness	Corrosion resistance	Cost
Titanium	4.5	Low	High	Very high
Aluminium alloy	2.8	Low	Low	Moderate
Melamine resin	1.5	Moderate	High	Low
Glass	2.5	Very high	High	Low

Figure 6

a) Titanium and the aluminium alloy both have a metallic structure.
    Suggest **one** similarity you would expect in the physical properties of titanium
    and the aluminium alloy, other than the properties mentioned in the table.
    Explain your answer in terms of their structure and bonding.

    ....

    ....

    ....

    [2]

b) Titanium is a transition metal.
    Give **two** typical properties of transition metals which are **not** common to all metals.

    1. ....

    2. ....

    [2]

c) A camping supplies company wants to make low-cost cups for people to use on camping holidays.
    Suggest which of the materials listed in **Figure 6** would be **most** suitable for this purpose.
    Explain your answer.

    ....

    ....

    ....

    ....

    ....

    ....

    ....

    ....

    [4]

    [Total 8 marks]

9 Rubidium is an element from Group 1 of the periodic table.
Fluorine is an element from Group 7.
Rubidium metal, Rb, and fluorine gas, F_2, react violently to produce a single product.

Grade 6-7

a) Write a balanced symbol equation for the reaction of rubidium metal and fluorine gas.

....

[2]

b) What type of bonding exists in the product of this reaction?

....

[1]

c) Would you expect the product of this reaction to have a high or low melting point?
Explain your answer in terms of the forces within the compound.

....

....

....

....

[2]

[Total 5 marks]

10 A student reacts chlorine water reacts with potassium iodide solution according to the following reaction.

Grade 6-7

$$Cl_{2\,(aq)} + 2KI_{(aq)} \rightarrow 2KCl_{(aq)} + I_{2\,(aq)}$$

a) Chlorine water is corrosive.
State **one** safety precaution that the student should take when carrying out the reaction.

....

[1]

b) Describe what the student would observe when he
added chlorine water to potassium iodide solution.

....

[1]

c) Explain why this reaction takes place.
Give your answer in terms of the reactivity of the elements involved.

....

....

[2]

d) Write a balanced ionic equation for the reaction between chlorine and potassium iodide.

....

[2]

[Total 6 marks]

11 Some elements have several different isotopes. Look at **Figure 7**.
It shows the percentage of the atoms of some elements that exist as each of their isotopes.

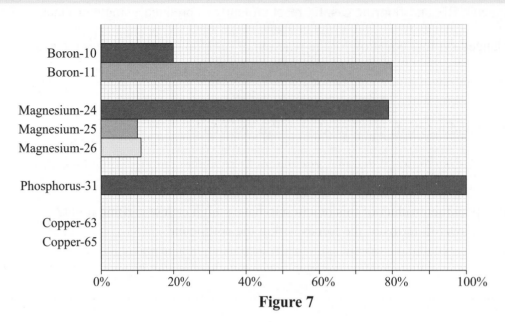

Figure 7

a) 69% of copper atoms are copper-63 and the rest are copper-65.
Complete **Figure 7** by adding bars for the two isotopes of copper.

[2]

b) Explain why the relative atomic mass of phosphorus is a whole number,
while the relative atomic masses of boron, magnesium and copper are not.

....

....

....

....

....

....

[3]

c) Use **Figure 7** to calculate the relative atomic mass of magnesium.
Give your answer to three significant figures.

relative atomic mass = ...

[4]

[Total 9 marks]

12 A student has a sample of sodium sulfate, Na_2SO_4, with a mass of 34.08 g.
How many oxygen atoms are in the sample, to 4 significant figures?

(relative atomic masses: Na = 23, S = 32, O = 16)

☐ **A** 1.442×10^{23} atoms   ☐ **C** 1.015×10^{24} atoms

☐ **B** 5.779×10^{23} atoms   ☐ **D** 1.442×10^{24} atoms

[Total 1 mark]

13 Aluminium can be obtained by electrolysis of the ore bauxite, Al_2O_3. **(Grade 6-7)**

The overall equation for this reaction is:

$$2Al_2O_{3\,(l)} \rightarrow 4Al_{(l)} + 3O_{2\,(g)}$$

a) Explain why this reaction is an example of a redox reaction.

....

....
[1]

b) Write a half equation to show the reaction that occurs at the cathode.

....
[2]

c) A scientist carries out an experiment where aluminium oxide is electrolysed.
The scientist starts off with 40.8 g of pure aluminium oxide.
Predict the mass of aluminium she can extract from this mass of electrolyte.
(relative atomic masses: Al = 27, O = 16)

mass = ... g
[4]

d) Iron can be extracted from its ores by heating with carbon.
Explain why this method is **not** suitable for the extraction of aluminium from its ore.

....

....

....
[2]

e) In the UK, some metals are widely recycled. Give **two** advantages of recycling metals.

....

....
[2]

[Total 11 marks]

14 A scientist wants to produce a batch of aluminium sulfate for an experiment.
She plans to do this by reacting aluminium with an excess of sulfuric acid.
A chemical supplier offers three options to provide the quantity of aluminium she needs. **(Grade 6-7)**

Which of these options will allow the scientist to complete her reaction in the **shortest** time?

☐ **A** 1 aluminium cube with side length 8 cm.

☐ **B** 8 aluminium cubes, each with side length 4 cm.

☐ **C** 64 aluminium cubes, each with side length 2 cm.

☐ **D** They will all take the same length of time.

[Total 1 mark]

15 The equation for the Haber process is: $N_2 + 3H_2 \rightleftharpoons 2NH_3$
In the Haber Process, the forwards reaction is exothermic. Which of the following will result in an **increase** in the yield of ammonia during the Haber process? Tick **one** box.

Grade 6-7

☐ **A** Decreasing the pressure.　　☐ **C** Increasing the temperature.

☐ **B** Adding a catalyst.　　☐ **D** Removing ammonia from the reaction chamber.

[Total 1 mark]

16 Andre wants to prepare a sample of copper carbonate, $CuCO_3$.
To do this, he mixes solutions of sodium carbonate, Na_2CO_3, and copper chloride, $CuCl_2$.

Grade 6-7

a) Complete the following equation for Andre's reaction by adding state symbols.

$$Na_2CO_3 \,(\ldots\ldots) + CuCl_2 \,(\ldots\ldots) \rightarrow CuCO_3 \,(\ldots\ldots) + 2NaCl \,(\ldots\ldots)$$

[1]

b) When the reaction is complete, Andre wants to obtain a pure sample of copper carbonate.

   i) Andre suggests using crystallisation to separate copper carbonate from the reaction mixture. Explain why this would be an **unsuitable** method.

   ....

   ....

   ....

   [2]

   ii) Suggest a suitable method Andre could use to obtain a pure sample of copper carbonate from the reaction mixture.

   ....

   [1]

c) Calculate the atom economy of Andre's reaction to make copper carbonate.
Give your answer to two significant figures.
(relative atomic masses: Na = 23, C = 12, O = 16, Cu = 63.5, Cl = 35.5)

atom economy = ...%
[5]

d) By using a suitable method to separate the mixture, Andre obtains 21.51 g of copper carbonate. Using the masses of reactants, Andre calculated that should have produced 28.68 g of copper carbonate. Calculate his percentage yield of copper carbonate.

percentage yield = ...%
[3]

[Total 12 marks]

Mixed Questions

17 A hydrogen-oxygen fuel cell is a type of electrical cell.

a) Hydrogen is the fuel used in the hydrogen-oxygen fuel cell.

 i) Suggest **two** advantages associated with using hydrogen as a fuel instead of fossil fuels.

....

....

[2]

 ii) Suggest **two** disadvantages of using hydrogen as a fuel instead of fossil fuels.

....

....

[2]

b) The reaction that occurs in a hydrogen-oxygen fuel cell is shown below.

$$2H_2 + O_2 \rightarrow 2H_2O$$

Figure 8 shows the energy of the bonds involved in this reaction.

Bond	Bond Energy (kJ mol⁻¹)
O=O	498
H–H	436
O–H	463

Figure 8

Calculate the energy change for the reaction which takes place in the hydrogen-oxygen fuel cell.

energy change = ... kJ mol⁻¹

[3]

c) A scientist recorded the amount of oxygen used by a fuel cell over a certain period of time.
The quantity of oxygen used occupied 156 dm³ at room temperature and pressure.
Calculate the mass of water produced if all of the oxygen reacted.

1 mole of gas occupies 24 dm³ at room temperature and pressure.
(relative atomic masses: H = 1, O = 16)

mass = ... g

[4]

[Total 11 marks]

Mixed Questions

18 Many different chemical substances are carbon based.

a) Carbon nanotubes are a type of nanoparticle. Explain what a nanoparticle is.
Explain why carbon nanotubes have different properties to bulk carbon.

....

....

[2]

b) Graphite is a material made of carbon that has applications as a lubricant.
Explain how the structure of graphite makes it suitable for this use.

....

....

....

[3]

c) i) Put the carbon-based substances butane, diamond and poly(propene)
in order of melting point, from **highest** to **lowest**. Explain your answer.

Order: ....

Explanation: ....

....

....

....

[5]

ii) Which of the substances from c) i) would be most suitable for using in drill bits?
Explain your answer with reference to the bonding in your chosen material.

....

....

....

[3]

[Total 13 marks]

19 Hydrochloric acid, HCl, reacts with aluminium.
The reaction produces aluminium chloride, $AlCl_3$, and hydrogen gas.

$$6HCl_{(aq)} + 2Al_{(s)} \rightarrow 2AlCl_{3\,(aq)} + 3H_{2\,(g)}$$

Calculate the volume of hydrogen gas produced when 162 g of aluminium is added to an excess
of hydrochloric acid. Assume the reaction takes place at room temperature and pressure.
1 mole of gas occupies 24 dm^3 at room temperature and pressure.
(relative atomic masses: H = 1, Al = 27)

volume = ... dm^3

[Total 3 marks]

CEQ41

Mixed Questions